T0157551

Towards the Realization of World Peace

Towards the Realization of World Peace

Edeh as a Role Model

EMMANUEL M. P. EDEH

Edited by
Sr. Purissima Egbepkalu SJS Ph.D,
Senior Lecturer
Dept. of Philosophy,
Madonna University, Nigeria.

authorHOUSE®

AuthorHouse™
1663 Liberty Drive
Bloomington, IN 47403
www.authorhouse.com
Phone: 1 (800) 839-8640

© 2015 Emmanuel M. P. Edeh. All rights reserved.

Author Credits: Edited by Sr. Purissima Egbepkalu SJS Ph.D

Royalty: Copyright Owner

No part of this book may be reproduced, stored in a retrieval system, or
transmitted by any means without the written permission of the author.

Published by AuthorHouse 06/03/2015

ISBN: 978-1-5049-1386-7 (sc)
ISBN: 978-1-5049-1385-0 (e)

Library of Congress Control Number: 2015908075

Print information available on the last page.

Any people depicted in stock imagery provided by Thinkstock are models,
and such images are being used for illustrative purposes only.
Certain stock imagery © Thinkstock.

This book is printed on acid-free paper.

Because of the dynamic nature of the Internet, any web addresses or links contained in
this book may have changed since publication and may no longer be valid. The views
expressed in this work are solely those of the author and do not necessarily reflect the
views of the publisher, and the publisher hereby disclaims any responsibility for them.

TABLE OF CONTENTS

List of Contributors..ix

General Introduction xi

Chapter 1 Edeh's Philosophy and Human Rights: Leading to
World Peace...1

    Introduction 1

    Human Rights Defined......................................2

    History Excursus of Human Rights.............................3

    The Foundation of Human Rights 5

    Human Dignity: A Review of Thoughts of Thinkers 7

    Human Dignity in the Scripture 8

    Dignity of Man and Edeh's Philosophy 9

    Practical consequences of Human Dignity in Edeh's
Philosophy.. 10

    Human Rights in the Light of Edeh's Philosophy.......... 12

    Conclusion 13

Chapter 2 World Peace Through Medical Services: the Philosophy
Behind Fr. E.M.P. Edeh's Medical Institutions................. 14

    Introduction 14

    Nigerian People and Medical Challenges........................15

    The Rural Areas, Rural Dwellers and Medical
Challenges 17

    Maternal Mortality..19

Chapter 3 Impact of Edehism on the Development of Girl-Child
Education 29

    Introduction 29

    Concept of Girl-Child Education 30

Cultures and Traditions that Perpetuate Gender
Differences in Education: 31

Functions of Girl-Child Education 32

Educated Women are Concerned with Family
Planning 33

The Concept of Edehism 33

Being "Good That Is" 33

Concept of Development 34

Theoretical Framework 35

Edeh's Philosophy of Practical and Effective Doing
(Charity) and Girl-Child Education 35

Conclusion 37

Chapter 4   Education and Women Empowerment in Edeh's
Practical Philosophy; Implications for Global Peace 39

Introduction 40

Edeh's Philosophy: A Peace Model 41

Edeh's Pragmatic Philosophy: A Precursor of the
United Nations Millennium Development Goals
(MDGs) 42

Education in Edeh: A Catalyst for Constructive
Development 43

Education and Women Empowerment in Edeh:
Effective Tools for Actualization of Gender Equality
and Promotion of Peace 47

Global Peace as an Impossible-Possible Project:
Edeh's Pragmatic Philosophical Logic 49

Conclusion 50

Chapter 5   African Philosophy of Life for Man and Woman
Everywhere 52

Introduction 52

Divinely Inspired Beginning: 53

Edehism, African Philosophy of Life and Being -
"I Have a Dream" 58

Chapter 6 The Charism of Fr. Emmanuel Edeh, C.S.Sp.,
A Man of Many Parts, The Gift for World Peace 60

Conclusion 62

Chapter 7 Edeh's Philosophy of Thought and Action (Eptaism)
as Foundation for Cross-Cultural Relationships and
World Peace... 64

Introduction 64

EPTAISM, Cross Cultural Relationships and
World Peace... 66

Conclusion 69

Chapter 8 Edeh's University Education and Social Stability.............. 70

Introduction 70

Role of University Education 72

Fr. Edeh and the Establishment of Tertiary Institutions 73

Merits of Edeh's University Institutions...................... 75

Summary and Conclusion 78

Chapter 9 Edeh's Philosophy in Moral Education and World Peace 79

Introduction 79

Moral Education for the Achievement of World Peace....... 80

Edeh's Philosophy of Thought and Action in Moral
Education: A Practical Approach to World Peace........... 81

Conclusion 85

Chapter 10 Engineering Education for Our Time: Fr. Edeh's
Singular Contribution to World Peace Through
Technological Development 86

Introduction 86

Concluding Remarks.. 91

Chapter 11 The Topology of Peace in the Information Age 93

Chapter 12 Education and Development in Africa: The Role of
    Fr. Edeh - A Leading Figure in World Peace 108

   Establishment of Museum of Charms & Fetish
   Objects 109

   Edeh's Charity Peace Model is characterized by: 110

   Conclusion 113

General Conclusion 115

Bibliography 119

LIST OF CONTRIBUTORS

Tobias Ozioko and Joseph Mbave

Sr. Dr. Yves Iwuamadi, SJS.

Dr. Regina Acholonu

Sr. Purissima Egbepkalu SJS Ph.D

Dr. Charles C. Umeh, M. Phil. Ph.D.

Fr. Prof. Augustine Onyeneke C.S.Sp., Ph.D.

Dr. Mike Ike Okwudili, Ph.D.

Prof. Alumode Bernard Ede, Ph.D.

Anyahuru Adah

Prof. Onyema E. Uzoamaka, Ph.D.

Dr. Atabong T. Agendia-Abanda, Ph.D.

Mrs. Kumkum Mathur.

GENERAL INTRODUCTION

It is an indisputable fact that our global village is in want of peace. When you get up from your bed in the morning and spare some attention to a radio or television station or rub your mind on pages of newspapers, you are bound to be confronted with the same sad and unfortunate news of violence, crime, wars, killings, racism, political/economic exploitation, students' unrest, and what have you. It is almost if not impossible to recall a single day that ran its course without any of the aforementioned calamities showcasing its ugly face in human society. Without fear of contradiction, no former generation has had to experience so much bad news as we face today. This constant awareness of fear, terror, and tension in our world should make any sensitive and concerned person seriously question the survival of our generation.

Ironically, most of these serious problems emanate from the more industrialized and the so-called advanced societies. This implies that science and technology have worked wonders in many fields, but the basic problem of man, which is lack of inner peace, remains. Again, there is unprecedented literacy, yet this universal education does not seem to have fostered goodness but only mental restlessness and discontent instead. There is no doubt about the increase in our material progress and technology, but somehow this is not sufficient as we have not yet succeeded in bringing about the most important and indispensable value that the human society yearns for -which is an internal peace and happiness; and this can only be achieved through an authentic perception of the real identity of man as *mmadi*—the good that is.

This notion of man as the good that proceeds from the African philosophy which does not see man as wolf to another but portrays man as good since he participates in the goodness of his creator (God). This same philosophy as articulated by Edeh is as practical as it is theoretical; hence, it does not only speculate about the goodness of man but also seeks the actualization of those realities that can actually bring about the welfare of man whom God as Chineke creates and as Osebuluwa cares for. Our mission for human welfare therefore according to Edeh is imperative as it behooves us to love and care for our fellow human in the same manner God cares for us and by so doing engender peace and co-existence in the world.

This piece of work is a calculated attempt aimed at showcasing how Fr. Edeh through his Philosophy of Thought and Action (EPTAISM) has put in place realities that have abolished violence and installed peace, realities that have condemned dehumanization and enthroned the care and love for humanity.

In Chapter One, which hinges on Edeh's Philosophy and Human Rights, Mbave Joseph and Ozioka Tobias are of the opinion that one of the major factors that keep the world from being united is the presumption of racial superiority which goes with the desire to conquer and convert thereby jeopardizing the inherent human right of all people created in the image of God *Imago Dei*. The only way to break through the barriers of distinction that seem to exist among us is through a clear understanding of human rights as epitomized in Edeh's philosophy. This philosophy insists that hatred does not cease by creating hatred at any time. On the contrary, hatred is ceased by love; insisting that those who know this as preached and practiced in Elele in the Centre for Peace Justice and Reconciliation, established by Fr. Edeh, their quarrels cease at once.

Chapter Two takes up the philosophical reasons behind Edeh's establishment of medical institutions. Here it is seen that proper health care in most African countries is something strictly reserved for the minute, privileged members of the society. Aware of the fact that sickness hampers the well-being of man and deprives him of peace, Edeh, who insists that man is good and must be cared for, went out of his way and established numerous health institutions where people, especially the disadvantaged, are medically taken care of, thereby bringing peace in their hearts which cannot be found in ill-health.

Chapter Three deals with an issue that is presently attracting serious attention in the International Society—the Girl-Child Education with the title "Impact of Edehism in the Development of Girl-Child Education: Great Achievement to World Peace." The research explores the fact that thinking of world peace without gender equality in education is a mirage. It goes on to showcase how Prof. Edeh through his numerous educational institutions has not only shown the capabilities and potentialities of the

Girl-Child but also set in place realities that support women's education and empowerment gearing towards their emancipation and consequently enthroning peace in our world.

Again, the old philosophy that enthrones and favours a male -dominated society is presented and dragged to the judgment seat of sound reasoning where the female gender seeks convincing explanations for the dehumanisation of women in homes, work places, in terms of appointment etc. Edeh's practical philosophy maintains that all human beings with no exception are created in the image of God and consequently deserves respect without discrimination. By practically implementing this in his daily activities, Edeh has gone a long way in reducing tension between the two genders by providing a pragmatic tool to achieving the desired global peace.

On the other hand, Edeh's Philosophy of Thought and Action has already taken an international dimension in which researchers all over the world have discovered a new pattern of thought for sustainability of peace and progress in the world. It is a pattern of thought that could bring to an end all the shedding of human blood all over the nations of the modern world.

Using Edehism as a school of thought, one here x-rays how Edeh, through his Philosophy of Thought and Action (EPTAISM), has pursued the well-being of human with keen interest. Edeh's concept of man as good led him to concretize his thought process, which has led him (Edeh) to construct realities that further the course of man as good thereby bringing peace to our troubled world.

The section of this work entitled *University Education in Edeh and Social Stability* opines that education is the backbone of individual empowerment, which enables nations to thrive socially, economically, politically, and religiously. According to this, Edeh has succeeded in using the university education as an epitome of social stability as he inculcates in the youth who go through his tertiary institutions the mission to always aspire for peace wherever they find themselves and in this manner spread peace across the globe.

Edeh's philosophy as it affects the moral formation of the youth is supreme. By insisting on deep-rooted moral education in his educational institutions,

Edeh has succeeded in his effort in engineering and fostering peace in the lives of millions of people.

On engineering education and technological development, one maintains that through EPTAISM, Edeh has set the engineering faculty of the prestigious Madonna University on a very exciting mission to rescue Nigeria technologically. This paradigm shift in engineering education based on Edeh's Philosophy of Thought and Action definitely will bring about the overdue awaited development which will in turn bring peace in the hearts of our people especially those in anyway involved in engineering and technology.

The discussion on *Topology of Peace in the Information Age* asserts that using the structure arranged in all network topologies, Edeh has successfully established peace among millions of individuals and families. Accordingly, the hierarchical topological arrangement of Edeh's charity peace model shows all Edeh's establishments through which this peace has been achieved via giving health to frustrated patients who eventually took to the Pilgrimage Centre as their home and will never return to their places of birth, educating the less privileged and dropouts, accommodating those totally rejected and abandoned by the society, and in this manner giving peace to millions of troubled hearts.

Finally, Mrs. Kumkum Mathur from India states in clear terms that one cannot hold any reasonable discussion on world peace without bringing Fr. Edeh to the centre of the picture

By his establishments, Edeh in no small measure impacts the lives of millions of people giving them the peace that has eluded men and women of our time.

It is our earnest expectation that this piece of work, which came as a result of the presentations at the International Convention of Experts and Intellectuals on World Peace organised by Madonna University in November 2013, would for all time serve as a reference point for people of all ages who dream and work towards the realisation of world peace.

CHAPTER ONE

EDEH'S PHILOSOPHY AND HUMAN RIGHTS: LEADING TO WORLD PEACE

By Tobias Ozioko and Joseph Mbave

Abstract

An in-depth scrutiny makes apodictic the fact that the concept "human rights" is based on an understanding of the being: man. In his monumental work Towards An Igbo Metaphysics, Edeh espouses a philosophy of being that is not only akin to this understanding of man (at the base of human rights) but most importantly illuminates it. Being a doing philosophy, Edeh has not only theorized this concept of man but has set himself practicalising it. In the main, this work undertakes a study of Edeh's philosophy, its practical application in concrete human existence and its take on human rights.

Introduction

In recent times, there have been relentless efforts to propagate, uphold and protect human rights. This endeavour is not exclusive to the contemporary era. However, the intensity of the struggle in the recent past is exceptional. Cases of those who willingly underwent unspeakable torture and those who even sacrificed their lives to uphold the human rights for those who in some cases may not have met in person abound. These altruistic gestures accentuate the fact that human rights is of great importance. Regrettably, so many people still wallow in the pit of ignorance of these fundamental human rights. There is no gainsaying, to say the least, that a person who possesses an innumerable amount of treasure but is ignorant of it is as unfortunate and pitiable as a person who possesses nothing. Indeed, his case is more disheartening.

In like manner, a person who is ignorant of human rights cannot lay claim to them. Cognizant of the fact that many are not well-informed on this subject, an in-depth study of the aforementioned concept becomes pertinent. Edeh's Philosophy of Thought and Action (EPTAISM) enhances our understanding of these human rights. This is the case because the foundation on which human rights are built upon is akin to the foundation upon which Edeh's Philosophy of Thought and Action (EPTAISM) is built. Being a philosophy, EPTAISM has the advantage of possessing more clarified nuances. Being a doing philosophy, EPTAISM has been and continues to be realized in concrete human situations; its results speak for it. Using these added advantages of EPTAISM as *instrumentum laboris,* a succinct yet lucid elucidation of the human rights is arrived at. However, we shall first elucidate human rights and its foundation, after which we shall briefly discourse Edeh's philosophy and its foundation. Finally, we shall explore the links between the two.

Human Rights Defined

According to Beauchamp, T.L., "the expression 'human rights' is a recent label for what has traditionally been referred to as 'natural rights' or, in an older vernacular, 'rights of man'" (Beauchamp, T.L., 1982, p. 206). The nomenclature "human rights" preempts the meaning of the concept. They are rights that belong to the human species just because he is human. The rights emanate from the nature of man. In other words, the rights are inherent in human nature. The Office of the High Commissioner for Human Rights defines human rights as "rights inherent to all human beings, whatever our nationality, place of residence, sex, national or ethnic origin, colour, religion, language, or any other status" (OHCHR, 2013).For Tom Head, "the term 'human rights' refers to those rights that are considered universal to humanity, regardless of citizenship, residency status, ethnicity, gender, or other considerations" (Tom Head, 2013). Sepúlveda holds that human rights are "commonly understood as inalienable fundamental rights to which a person is inherently entitled simply because she or he is a human being."(Sepúlveda, 2004, p. 3) Since they are inherent in human nature, human rights are acclaimed to be universal and inalienable to man. To say that human rights are universal implies that wherever man exists, under whatever culture, he lives; in any geopolitical habitat, he finds himself; at whatever time in history he exists, these rights are privileges he ought to enjoy. Similarly, the assertion that human rights are inalienable connotes that since human rights are intrinsically connected to the nature of man, insofar as man remains man, he possesses those rights. The argument can be demonstrated thus, human rights can be alienated from man if man's nature can be alienated from him. However, since man's nature cannot be alienated from him, human rights cannot be alienated from man. In recent years, some philosophers have raised objections as to the validity of the universality and inalienability claim of the human rights.

History Excursus of Human Rights

As aforesaid, Beauchamp, T.L holds that human rights are a recent label for what has traditionally been referred to as natural rights. In Locke's opinion, natural rights have their footing in natural law. Hence, natural rights were deemed to pre-exist actual social and political systems by social contract theorists such as John Locke.

Thus, natural rights are considered ultimately valid whether or not they are recognized by any given political ruler or assembly. John Locke, a 17th century philosopher is a foremost proponent of this position. In his *Two Treatises of Government* (1688), Locke argued that "individuals possess natural rights, independently of the political recognition granted them by the state. These natural rights are possessed independently of, and prior to, the formation of any political community" (Andrew Fagan, 2005, accessed 13/4/2013 www.iep.utm.edu/hum-rts/). Locke argues that individuals had to entrust these rights to a leader for the sake of order and peace. This, according to Locke, is the emergence of political society. However, there are some inalienable rights which the individual cannot relinquish; rather the state has only but to protect these rights. Locke even went to the extent of advocating for rebellion against instituted government should they fail to protect these rights. These inalienable rights include life, liberty, and happiness. The import of this claim that rights predate political society is that the coming into being of natural rights coincides with the coming into being of man. In other words, natural rights are as old as man.

In history, men have grappled with the concept human rights. In different epochs, the concept has taken different names and shapes. Taking from Beauchamp, T.L., it was initially denoted with the name natural rights.

In France around 1789, it was legally recognized as the right of man. Nevertheless, "the term human rights probably came into use sometime between Paine's The Rights of Man and William Lloyd Garrison's 1831 writings in *The Liberator*, in which he stated that he was trying to enlist his readers in "the great cause of human rights."(Wikipedia, accessed 11/4/2013).

In different epochs, attempts have been made by different leaders and governments to promulgate a number of legal edicts that could be said to be precursors of and might have influenced the modern formulation of the concept of human rights. In 539 B.C., Cyrus the Great and his Persian army conquered the city of Babylon. He however "freed the slaves, declared that all people had the right to choose their own religion, and established racial equality. These and other decrees were recorded on a baked-clay cylinder in the Akkadian language with cuneiform script. Known today as the Cyrus Cylinder, this ancient record has now been recognized as the world's first charter of human rights" (http://www.humanrights.com/ what-are-human-rights/brief-history/cyrus-cylinder.html, 20/4/2013). Other edicts include: The Magna Carta which was promulgated in the year 1215; The Petition of Right promulgated in 1628; The 1776 United States Declaration of Independence; The 1789 Declaration of the Rights of Man in France, the US Bill of Rights promulgated in 1791, et cetera. Finally, in the year 1948, the United Nations adopted a document, which today has attained the statute of the most important document on human rights. The document was simply titled *The Universal Declaration of Human Rights*.

The Universal Declaration of Human Rights came to light after the Second World War. The Second World War occasioned the most dreadful, appalling, horrendous, and abysmal atrocities against the human race; the outrageous massacre of war prisoners; the abominable genocide against the Jews; and many more regrettable crimes against humanity. The Hiroshima and Nagasaki bombings still echo blaring reproach to us.

It is against this pernicious reality that the world embarked on a search of panacea to ameliorate the horrid and despicable condition of a good number of the human family, which is the resultant effect of the Second World War. The search also aimed at providing means of forestalling the reenactment of similar occurrences in the future. Recognizing that a clear understanding of human rights was necessary to achieve this aim, the

United Nations, the universal body that was instituted after the Second World War to replace the League of Nations (still in quest for solution), was charged with the duty of codifying Human Rights. In 1948, they came up with the document *Universal Declaration of Human Rights*. Today this document is regarded as the most important document with regard to human rights.

The Foundation of Human Rights

The very first sentence of the introduction of the Universal Declaration of Human rights introduces the concept on which the edifice of human rights is erected. It reads, "Whereas recognition of the inherent dignity and of the equal and inalienable rights of all members of the human family is the foundation of freedom, justice and peace in the world..." (http://www.un.org/en/documents/udhr/index.shtml, accessed 11/4/2013). One can deduce from this opening statement that the Universal Declaration of Human Rights aims at bringing freedom, justice and peace in the world, but this can only be realized by the recognition of the inherent dignity of man. Note however that freedom, justice, and peace are at the service of human dignity. Thus, the dignity of man can be said to be the foundation of human rights. A study of the rest of the thirty articles of the Universal Declaration shows that they were enacted to define, restore, protect or to promote human dignity. In Donnelly's terms, "Human rights reflector at least analytically can be understood to reflect a particular specification of certain minimum preconditions for a life of dignity in the contemporary world." (Donnelly, 2009, p. 83)

Anthony Areji assent to the argument that human rights are founded on human dignity. He asserts that "the concept human rights, which has its basis on the dignity of human persons is as old as the homo sapiens, since human person is assumably born with inherent dignity" (Areji, 2007, p. 32).He asserts further that "human rights embody the basic standards without which people cannot realize their inherent dignity" (Areji, 2007, p.31). For Klaus Dicke, "human dignity functions with regard to the Universal Declaration of Human Rights as 'a formal, transcendental norm' or 'a formal background value'" (2002, pp.118, 120).

Nevertheless, some people have jettisoned the argument that human dignity is at the base of the conception of human rights. In this vein, Bagaric and James argue that "the concept of dignity is itself vacuous. As a legal or philosophical concept it is without bounds and ultimately is one incapable of explaining or justifying any narrower interests...the term is so elusive as to be virtually meaningless" (Bagaric and James 2006, p. 260). Acceding to the above, Davis posits that "the concept of human dignity does not give us enough guidance... it has different senses and often points us in opposite directions" (Davis 2007, p. 177).For Macklin, "dignity is a fuzzy concept, and appeals to dignity are often used to substitute for empirical evidence that is lacking or sound arguments that cannot be mustered" (Chalmers and Ida, 2007,p. 158; quoting Macklin, 2002,p. 212). The above arguments above imply that albeit the fact that "the concept of human dignity has become ubiquitous to the point of cliché" (Witte 2003, p. 121), it eludes comprehension.

Some others see human rights as "foundational, declaratory, and undefined" (Beyleveld and Brownsword, 1998, p. 663). Harris and Sulston see it as "a sort of axiom in the system or as a familiar and accepted principle of shared morality" (Harris and Sulston, 2004, p. 797). For Weisstub it is "a bedrock concept that resists definition in terms of something else" (Weisstub, 2002, p. 2; cf. Jack Donnelly, 2009, p. 81).

Nevertheless, one can posit in consonant with Jack Donnelly that human dignity is not an unanalyzable 'Ur-principle' (Witte, 2003, p. 119). "Although ambiguous, dignity is a signalling term that goes to the heart of what constitutes the quality of humanness" (Weisstub, 2002, p. 269). In Donnelly's opinion, "that ambiguity, however, arises not from any special lack of clarity or from the absence of deeper substantive foundations. Rather, it arises from the fact that for different people human dignity points to different deeper foundations" (Jack Donnelly, 2009, p. 82).In actual fact, both concepts; human rights and human dignity, can be said to enjoy a symbiotic relationship. Donnelly captures it better. In his words "Human rights reflect or at least analytically can be understood to reflect a particular specification of certain minimum preconditions for a life of dignity in the contemporary world. But our detailed understanding of human dignity is shaped by our ideas and practices of human rights. And the practice of human rights can be seen as justified, in some ultimate sense, by its production of beings able to live a life of dignity" (Donnelly, 2009, p. 83).

"Human rights thus go beyond the inherent dignity of the human person to provide mechanisms for realizing a life of dignity. Human rights both specify forms of life that are worthy of beings with inherent moral worth and provide legal and political practices to realize a life of dignity that vindicates the inherent worth of the human person" (Donnelly, 2009, p. 83).

Human Dignity: A Review of Thoughts of Thinkers

Following the critic that human dignity is vacuous and elusive as to be virtually meaningless (Bagaric and James) and the assertion that dignity is a fuzzy concept (Macklin) it becomes pertinent that we elucidate the concept human dignity.

Etymologically, the word dignity derives from the French dignite which in turn derives from the Latin noun dignitas; adjective dingus and verb dignor, these refer to the English word 'worth'. In the early Roman world "'dignity' was a term of hierarchical distinction, an attribute of a distinguished few (patricians or 'optimates') that marked them off from the vulgar masses"' (Donnelly, 2009, p. 15). Dignitas was the status that dignitaries had a quality that demanded reverence from the ordinary common person the vulgar, in the original meaning of that term" (Brennan and Lo, 2007, p. 44). According to Shell, "Dignity, in Latin usage, refers especially to that aspect of virtue or excellence that makes one worthy of honor which, as Aristotle put it, accompanies virtue as its crown" (Shell, 2003, p. 53). Englard captures it differently, "In Rome the original meaning of dignity (dignitas) referred to an acquired social and political status, implying, generally, important personal achievements in the public sphere and moral integrity" (Englard, 1999, p. 1904). From the above it is perspicuous that in the early Roman world, dignity was not perceived as a common feature of all men. Rather, it was an attribute given to a few based on their achievements either in morality according to Aristotelian sense or in the society.

In contrast, Kant's concept of human dignity is universalistic in nature. In Kantian philosophy, human dignity is not an attribute of a few. It is rather an inherent quality of every man. In fact, it is this inherent dignity of every man that underlies morality in Kantian ethics. Kant uses the German word *würde* which in his words means "an absolute inner worth" (Kant1991: 230 translated by M. Gregor Cambridge University press). In Kantian ethics, this inner worth of man is so valued that it comes second to nothing. Thus the categorical imperative which can be regarded as the bedrock of Kantian ethics: "Act in such a way that you treat humanity, whether in your own person or in the person of another, always at the same time as an end and never simply as a means" (Kant 1981:36 translated by J. Elingeon, Indiana Polis, Hakett Publisher).

Akin to Kant's inner worth, Gewirth defines human dignity as "a kind of intrinsic worth that belongs equally to all human beings as such, constituted by certain intrinsically valuable aspects of being human." (1992, p. 12, cf. Donnelly, 2009, p. 83) Similarly Joel Feinberg argues (akin to Kantian categorical imperative) that human dignity means "expressing an attitude the attitude of respect toward the humanity in each man's person." (1973, 94).

Human Dignity in the Scripture

The Hebrew word kavod, which translates dignity, honour, respect, or glory, appears in many passages of the Old Testament. However, the combination kvod Ha'adam (dignity of man) cannot be found in the scripture. Kavod is used as an attribute of God wherever it appeared. Nevertheless, the Scripture is a very rich source of human dignity. The concept *Imago Dei* found in the very first book of the Bible (Genesis) has served and continues to serve as a reference point in many discursions on human dignity.

> Genesis, Chapter 1, Verses 24-28: Let the earth produce every kind of living creature in its own species: cattle, creeping things and wild animals of all kinds. And so it was. God made wild animals in their own species, and cattle in theirs, and every creature that crawls along the earth in its own species. God saw that it was good. God said, "Let us make man in our own image, in the likeness of ourselves, and let them be masters of the fish of the sea, the birds of heaven, the

cattle, all the wild animals and all the creatures that creep along the ground." God created man in the image of himself, in the image of God, he created him, male and female he created them. God blessed them, saying to them, "Be fruitful, multiply, fill the earth and subdue it. Be masters of the fish of the sea, the birds of heaven and all the living creatures that move on earth."(New Jerusalem Bible)

To further accentuate the dignity of man, Psalms Chapter 8, Verses 4-6 reads, "What are human beings that you spare a thought for them, or the child of Adam that you care for him? Yet you have made him little less than a god, you have crowned him with glory and beauty, made him lord of the works of your hands, put all things under his feet..." (New Jerusalem Bible.)Thus, among other creatures of God, man holds a dignified position since he was made in the image of God. What is more, right from the beginning of creation, he was made master of all other creatures.

Dignity of Man and Edeh's Philosophy

"Edeh's philosophy as articulated in his opus magnum (Towards an Igbo Metaphysics) is a lived philosophy rather than a purely theoretical or scientific venture. It is a practical theoretical science." (Tobias in Melladu, 2012). While erudite scholars both within and outside the shores of the African continent engaged themselves in a debate to prove or disprove the existence of anything called African philosophy, Edeh went into doing the African philosophy. Consequent upon this, his opus magnum *Towards an Igbo Metaphysics* emerged. The aforementioned work has been described as a milestone in the history of thought.

An essential contribution of Edeh's philosophy stems from his understanding of man. Prior to the emergence of Edeh's opus magnum, different philosophers have rationalized on man and have attempted varied definitions of him: For Aristotle, man is a political animal; for Plato, he is an embodied soul; in Marxist philosophy, he is a social animal; according to Bloch, he is an utopic being, Cassier defined him as a symbol-making animal; Benjamin Franklin calls him tool-making animal (Homo-faber); in Paschal's parlance, man is a thinking reed. However, the problem with these attempts to define man is that the definitions are based on what he does and not on whom man is.

In contrast, Edeh's understanding of man is based on what man is not on what he does. According to Edeh, the understanding of being among the Igbo people of southeast Nigeria begins with their awareness of man. The above was arrived at via the analysis of his interview with Mazi Ede Oje. Ede Oje's response to his question "Kedu k' isi malu na ife di?" (How do you know that beings are?) was "Emegi ife ozo, amalum nkea maka na madu di, maka n anyi di." (I know this at least from the fact that human beings are; because we are.) (Edeh, 1985).

Edeh's concept of man stems from etymological analysis of the Igbo word for man. According to Edeh the Igbo name for man, *mmadu*, is an abridged form of *mmadi*. *Mmadi*, Edeh avers, is made up of two components: *Mma* meaning good, and *di*, which is a short form of *idi*, the verb *to be*. Man then as understood by the Igbo is *the good that is*. Why is man the good that is? To answer this question, Edeh goes back to the origin of man. Man is good because he is made by God. Edeh, however, insists that man is not good in se. It is only God who is good in se. The goodness of man is participatory. Man is "good that is" in the sense that having been created by God, he is a product of his maker. Hence, man shares in the being of his maker the highest good (Edeh, 2009). This underlies the dignity of man in Edeh's philosophy. Man is dignified not only that he is "good that is" but also that he participates, he shares in the being of the ultimate Being who is his maker.

Practical consequences of Human Dignity in Edeh's Philosophy

Edeh did not stop at articulating the dignity of man; he went into action to see that man lives a life worthy of his dignity. He asserts

> "If you accept man as "good that is," we must go ahead and do our best and establish or cause to establish realities that depict man as such, realities that are metaphysically focused towards uplifting man from his low state that tends to make man sub-human, i.e., the state that categorizes him as the sick, the suffering, the abjectly poor, the handicapped, the blind, deaf, and dumb, the crippled, etc., the helpless and uneducated youths and the abandoned, and also as of the families entirely shattered by conflicts, quarrels and wars. Hence, after articulating African thought pattern in Igbo Metaphysics as far

back as 1985, I did not stop there. Rather, from then I became deeply involved in the action and process of implementing the thoughts in realities." (Edeh, 2006, p. 5).

These conditions enumerated above (abject poverty, lack of education, sickness, conflict, i.e., lack of peace, handicap, etc.) tend to diminish the human dignity. In Edeh's parlance, they make man to live a "sub human" life. In his understanding, it behooves on man the "good that is" to help support (as Osebuluwa carries and supports the world) to support other "good that is" to live the dignified life of "good that is." Consequent upon this, Edeh has been deeply involved in the process of elevating man to his exalted dignity. He has established a numberless number of schools—both nursery, primary and tertiary institutions—to educate the uneducated and to give everybody the opportunity of getting quality education. In these schools, the abjectly poor, the handicapped and some who cannot pay the school fees are given scholarships. In addition to this there are schemes put in place in these institutions to help low-income earning parents pay for the school fees of their wards.

The area of health is another section in which Edeh has made so much impact. In fact, in the hospitals owned by him, there is a permanent column for those who cannot pay their bills. Furthermore, free treatment is given to all and sundry periodically. Retired priests, all Bishops, and old people are on regular free medication. Medical treatments worth millions of naira have been granted free of charge through this project, which has been going on for many years and will continue, please God.

Edeh, through his poverty-alleviating projects, has improved the living conditions of many. Periodically, especially on Easter Sundays and New year days, he shares money and food to the poor, the needy, and the abandoned. He, however, does not stop at this. He also provides jobs for thousands of people who are poor and jobless; thereby reducing the number of jobless poor people in the streets. Hence he does not only give money or material gifts to the poor but also provides a source of constant and stable income for them.

Human Rights in the Light of Edeh's Philosophy

Ab ovo, it is fitting that we remark that the circumstances that led to the emergence of the Universal Declaration of Human Rights is akin to the circumstances that spurred Edeh into action to uplift the dignity of man. We may recall that the pitiable condition of many, the sequel to the Second World War was a stimulant to the emergence of the Universal Declaration of Human rights. Similarly, the tragic condition of many, the sequel to the Nigerian civil war was a stimulant to the practicalization of Edeh's philosophy. Thus, he asserts

> "... when I returned from the United States of America to Nigeria, I was hit by the reality of human life in the society where millions of shattered and broken human beings were staggering out of the protracted and devastating Nigerian Civil War (also known as the Nigeria Biafran War). In the face of this existential reality, I could not just sit down only to speculate and rationalize. Rather I went ahead into action by intensifying my mission of practical and effective charity ... the result of African metaphysical thought pattern." (Edeh, 2006, pp. 7-8)

Observe that both Edeh and United Nations were concerned with the dignity of man. The existential realities sequel to the Wars was threatening the dignity of man; it left many in sub-human conditions. According to Donnelly, "Human rights reflect, or at least analytically can be understood to reflect, a particular specification of certain minimum preconditions for a life of dignity in the contemporary world" (Donnelly, 2009, p. 83). Donnelly also posits that human rights thus go beyond the inherent dignity of the human person to provide mechanisms for realizing a life of dignity. Human rights specify both forms of life that are worthy of beings with inherent moral worth and provide legal and political practices to realize a life of dignity that vindicates the inherent worth of the human person (cf. Donnelly, 2009, p. 83).

Edeh did not stop at setting "specification of certain minimum preconditions for a life of dignity in the contemporary world" nor did he stop at "providing rational mechanisms for realizing a life of dignity." He further effected these mechanisms and even today continues to effect them in concrete life situations of many; thus, perpetually uplifting the dignity of man.

Furthermore, Edeh's leadership model is reminiscent of the Universal Declaration of Human Rights, Article 21. In Article 21, Paragraph 3, the UHR states "The will of the people shall be the basis of the authority of government."Similarly, Edeh espouses and practicalizes a leadership model that enthrones the good of the people. This leadership model is known as "Servant-Leadership Model." In this model, the leader becomes the servant of the people. He does not lord it over them. In other words, he does not become autocratic. The good of the people enjoys a prime position in decision-making. Thus, Edeh asserts, "Here is a leadership structure that I evolved. I am actively involved with the people, sharing their feelings, considering the needs of the people above my own needs in decisions making" (Edeh, 2012, p. 11).

Conclusion

From the foregoing, it is perspicacious that Edeh's notion of being is founded on his understanding of man; man as dignified. Since his philosophy is metaphysical as can be deduced from the title of his magnus opus "Towards an Igbo Metaphysics," and metaphysics is principally the study of being, it can be said that Edeh's philosophy is founded on human dignity. Similarly, it is apodictic from the expositions above that human dignity is both the foundation and the propelling force of the Universal Declaration of Human Rights. Human rights as is articulated in the Universal Declaration of Human Rights specify and set up mechanisms for the realization of the inherent dignity of man. However, in addition to an articulate elucidation of human dignity, Edeh does not only set mechanisms for, but has actually caused to realize this life of dignity among many who were previously dehumanized by poverty, hunger, ignorance, oppression and dejection, insecurity, absence of peace, et cetera, through his practical and effective charity. This practical and effective charity also stems from and aims at restoring and elevating the dignity of man. Interestingly, Edeh not only embarks recently on his mission of practical and effective charity but also encourages others to do likewise through his other Mechanisms such as the Madonna International Charity Peace Award (MICPA) as well as his medical services and medical institutions. Through these and others, Edeh is paving way to the realization of world peace.

CHAPTER TWO

WORLD PEACE THROUGH MEDICAL SERVICES: THE PHILOSOPHY BEHIND FR. E.M.P. EDEH'S MEDICAL INSTITUTIONS

By Sr. Dr. Yves Iwuamadi, SJS

Abstract

The well-being of man and peace are seriously hampered by sickness and ill-health. Hence Fr. Edeh insisting that man is good and deserves care has established numerous health institutions in which people, especially the disadvantaged, are medically cared for thereby engendering peace in their hearts.

Introduction

The question of health, that is being healthy or sick, is very central to the existence of every human being in the world. People would do everything possible in order to be healthy and to avoid everything that can make them to lose it. This is because they know from experience that good health is like the basis or foundation on which most of the other activities of life depend. Whoever contributes to making us healthy really contributes to our life in a very significant way. As it were, on a healthy body lies a healthy mind and on a healthy mind and body there we find peace. Consequently, one of the very fundamental ways through which Fr. Edeh has contributed to world peace is through the establishment of medical institutions and the training of medical personnel that provide medical services and health care to people particularly to the needy. This very claim can be supported by a lot of facts. It is interesting to note that his whole idea or philosophy that greater peace can be brought to the world by responding to human medical problems started as far back as the earliest period of his public ministry. Moreover, the continuity of this philosophy tells us that it was not a chance product in the first place and that he was not making any mistakes at all.

This research is aimed at highlighting the various ways and the degrees to which Fr. Edeh has contributed to world peace through the instrumentality of the medical institutions established by him, the medical personnel produced through these institutions and the various services rendered by them. We intend to begin this project by first examining the context in which Fr. Edeh found himself; namely Nigeria (Africa) and its populace, which made him to adopt the philosophy of peace through good health. Without some awareness of the peculiarities of health and medical conditions of majority of Nigerians, it would be difficult for us to understand and appreciate how Fr. Edeh's establishment of institutions for medical services and health care contribute to world peace.

Nigerian People and Medical Challenges

Nigeria, the so-called giant of Africa, is a big nation with a thick population of over 150 million people.

She is blessed with human and natural resources, anatomically endowed people dogged and resilient in nature.

She got her political independence in 1960 and became a republic in 1963 and ever since then has struggled to maintain her integrity as a sovereign nation. It is a fact known to everybody that the existence of this young Nation has been seriously challenged by so many factors such asethnicism, religious conflicts, corruption, nepotism, bad leadership, political instability, and sometimes sheer ignorance which culminated in the civil war that lasted about 30 months (nearly 3years, 6th July 1967 to 13th January 1970). During this war, many atrocities were committed such as rape, killings, betrayals and suspicions, which helped to give rise to deeper hatred, tension and intolerance in society. As a result of these, man became a wolf to another as tension among ethnic groups became strong and severe that political offices were given not on the basis of personal worth but on tribal affinity and affiliation.

Ever since the civil war, the struggle had continued taking the nation into many years of military ruler-ship, punctuated by intermittent change of governments through coup d'états. One could say fortunately, the military hegemony came to an end about 13years ago and giving way to a democratically elected government which does not work because in most cases the elections are rigged, votes are manipulated and allotted to undeserving and unworthy politicians. This has been the experience until now. So far, there is no doubt to any Nigerian that there is a huge difference between the military rule and democracy, nevertheless, Nigeria has continued to labour under serious challenges of bad governance. This has made corruption, insecurity of life and property, lack of employment for the youth and very low quality of life as almost part and parcel of our story.

Our youth who had no past because of the war and its aftermath, are miserable in the present day and apparently do not have a promising future. In the northern part of Nigeria, the youth are street urchins fighting at the slightest provocation of ethno- religious insults, while the youth in the south are kidnappers who are used to either kidnap for money or bomb innocent people or oil installations. Able-bodied Nigerian youth die of thirst in the Sahara desert or drown in Mediterranean where they are trying to run away from their fatherland to other countries where they hope to have better conditions of living. Those who remain behind in the country walk the streets of Nigeria without jobs. The politicians privatize everything Nigeria has and from behind they buy them up. This is why we are 'Green but not fertile'.

Therefore, given all these, it is not surprising that the people of the so-called highly blessed, rich and endowed giant of Africa, namely NIGERIA are suffering from poverty and misery which make some of them sometimes to desire the return of our country to the colonial masters.

One of the areas of life in Nigeria where this poverty and misery is highly manifested is in the area of health. As we know, Nigeria is one of the countries in the world that is strongly associated with the green colour; we find this as the dominant colour in the national flag. Green is usually associated with fertility because green vegetation enhances photosynthesis, which ultimately results to abundant and fruitful harvest. Green is also associated with life and good health. It sounds funny when one is awakened with the fact that these Nigerian people, who are supposed to be endowed with fruitful and abundant good health, die in thousands out of preventable diseases.

These preventable diseases send Nigerians to hospitals where there is paucity of trained healthcare personnel, drugs and other infrastructures. Today, there are more challenges which prompt the recurrent industrial disputes in our tertiary hospitals while the doctors in recent time are easy targets for kidnappers. Poor conditions of service for doctors and nurses make brain-drain a big problem; many nurses have gone abroad searching for greener pastures while the remaining are waiting for their turn. Statistics show that the Sub-Saharan Africa including Nigeria has the highest maternal and infant mortality rates in the world. In the meantime, our leaders who are supposed to work hard in solving these problems at hand prefer spending billions of naira or dollars or euro treating their catarrh and headaches abroad while the future generations are dying of preventable diseases. The Nigerian health institution and services are substandard yet it is not within the reach of the poor people who need it most. The institutions and the services they render are better described as epileptic and sick and this is not surprising when the whole country is swimming in the ocean of fake drugs in spite of the serious fight being put up by the National Agency for Food Drug Administration and control (NAFDAC) to eradicate it. Most drugs are either expired or carrying reprinted dates and the perpetrators of these crimes against humanity do not mind the dangers which their actions constitute to human lives. As a result, even a good number of our teaching hospitals are mere consulting rooms, "green but not fertile." Put simply, our health system appears hopeless and helpless and it is needless to say that the area and people mostly affected by this mess are the rural places and rural dwellers.

The Rural Areas, Rural Dwellers and Medical Challenges

Not minding the rapid growth of cities in Nigeria and the constant migration of people from villages to the urban areas, the majority of Nigerians still live in rural areas. There is usually a very huge distinction between the urban and rural areas in terms of basic amenities and standard of living. Typical rural areas are places where one can scarcely find good roads, effective means of transportation and communication, potable water, electricity, big shops or pharmacies. Medically speaking, some rural areas are dead zones in the sense that what is within their reach are mainly inexperienced medical personnel who most times administer either overdose or under dose drugs to patients, quack chemist-shop-dealers and of course most of us know what transpires when a square peg is being forced into a round hole; it is as bad as that.

The people we are talking about here are the abjectly poor, non-literate, vulnerable human beings but yet created in the same image and likeness of our God. Statistically, most people who fall within this group of victims are women of child-bearing age, children and the aged. They are medically ignorant and the women among them cannot even differentiate between being in labour and normal quickening during pregnancy. The majority of them do not know much about possible complications connected with pregnancy or what it means to be hypertensive, eclamptic, prolonged/obstructed labour, cephalo-pelvic disproportion, gestational diabetes, obstetric hemorrhage, complications of unsafe abortion, asthma etc. The so-called Local Birth Attendants who are usually at their service during child-birth continue manipulating their pregnancy until either luck is on their side and a live baby is delivered or the baby remain still birth or both mother and child meet untimely death in her hands. Such incidents, which are regular occurrences in our villages, can be attributed to sheer ignorance, lack of prior education or enlightenment, no antenatal care, non-availability of health workers, inadequate skilled attendants, inadequate supply of equipment and drugs.

Unfortunately, the government is not doing much to alleviate the medical problems of the rural dwellers. More so, the lack of basic amenities in these areas does not make them attractive for doctors and pharmacists to build hospitals and pharmacies there. Can we say something more on maternal death?

Maternal Mortality

Maternal and of course infant mortality count among the major health challenges facing Nigerians particularly those who live in the rural areas. By maternal mortality, we mean the death of a woman during pregnancy or within 42 days of termination of the pregnancy irrespective of the site and duration of such pregnancy, from causes related to, or aggravated by pregnancy or its management and not from incidental or accidental causes. Maternal mortality rate is equal to maternal death/live birth x 100,000. Based on this calculation, the Sub Sahara Africa has the highest maternal mortality rate in the world. It is really like a cankerworm that has eaten and continues to eat so deeply into the fabrics of the health of women in Nigeria. Let us consider some of these factors:

1. Medical Factors:

Obstetrics haemorrhage,
Ectopic Pregnancy,
Puerperal sepsis,
Pre-eclampsia,
Prolonged / Obstructed labour,
Complications of unsafe abortion,
Anesthetic procedures.

2. Sociocultural and Economic Factors:

Lack of women empowerment,
Poverty,
Poor Nutrition,
Ignorance / Non-literacy,
Religious belief,
Harmful traditional practices e.g. Northern norms of first delivery at home.

3. Health Service Factors:

Lack of access to essential obstetric care,
Lack of access to family counselling and services,
Non-availability of health workers for essential obstetric care,
Inefficient transport and communication services.

4. Reproductive Health Factors:

Underage at first birth, that is, less than 18years,
Too old, that is, more than 35years,
Too many deliveries, that is, greater than 5 children,
Too frequent deliveries, spacing less than 2years,
Other co-morbidities, like a patient with heart failure.

An average Nigerian with his low income cannot afford the services offered by good hospitals. In Nigeria, there is no existing effective health insurance for the citizens. By implication, every man or woman sees to his or her medical needs. In most developed nations, medical services and health care are provided under the insurance schemes. With the absence of workable insurance schemes and the inability of most people to provide for their medical needs the result is simple, many people suffer and die for lack of medical attention.

In the 21st century, many women in Nigeria still die during child bearing. Consequently maternal and infant mortality is still rated high. For example, gestational diabetes and hypertension. Often times they come to hospital only when their cases are so critical with poor prognosis or are as good as death. As we know, health care is not only about giving out medication; it's also about educating and enlightening people about their health. Even in this area of health education, it is obvious that a good number of Nigerians are deficient. Many do not even know what it means to be diabetic or have blood pressure or other similar diseases. This is made worse by the fact that many people are still deeply rooted in the African belief system that attributes most sicknesses to spiritual causes. This is the situation into which Fr. Edeh was born, brought up, and called to serve.

What comes to mind immediately is to unravel the mystery or to explain how Fr. Edeh was able to take a kind of distancing from this context to the extent that he saw it as a problem or challenge to be addressed and to occupy him as mission to humanity. Permit me, therefore, to reflect briefly on the life of Fr. Edeh particularly as it concerns the issues in question.

Put simply, we want to explain how Fr. Edeh's philosophy of mediating peace in the world through the provision of medical facilities and services came to be born.

5. The Making of Fr. Edeh

Reverend Father Professor Emmanuel M.P. Edeh C.S.Sp., hails from Akpugo in Nkanu West Local Government Area of Enugu State, Nigeria. He was born on 20 May 1947 to the family of late Mr. and Mrs. Joseph and Elizabeth Ani Onovo. His primary education was in his hometown from 1955 to 1962. His junior seminary formation was in the Holy Ghost Juniorate Ihiala from 1963 to 1967 and he completed his novitiate and philosophy studies from 1968 to 1970. His theological studies were at Bigard Memorial Seminary Enugu and in the year 1976 on 19 April, Easter Monday he was ordained a Catholic priest of the Holy Ghost Congregation in his hometown by the late Bishop Godfrey Mary Paul Okoye C.S.Sp.

The spirituality and charism of the Holy Ghost Congregation where Fr. Edeh was formed and to which he belongs played a great role in shaping him to be the type of person he is. Their Congregation is dedicated to the Holy Spirit under the patronage of the Immaculate Heart of Mary. The Holy Spirit is called the Father of the Poor. The members of the Holy Ghost Congregation are those who dedicate themselves to the services of the poor, the less privileged and the abandoned. We can see a strong link between the nature and activities of the Holy Spirit and the charism of the Holy Ghost Congregation and the philosophy of Fr. Edeh especially in the area of medical services.

From the first day of his ordination, he was filled with the inspiration and zeal for what he often calls his mission of practical and effective charity, which is holistic care for the sick, and suffering, the handicapped, the abjectly poor and the abandoned, and providing proper education for the troubled youths of modern society. He finds time to feed these poor people by himself, showing a concrete living of the existential dictates of practical and effective charity expressed in the poor, the sick and suffering people within and beyond the country.

In his words, Edeh stated, "My mission of practical and effective charity led to the establishment of realities that have been successful in finding peace and reconciliation to the African Society; taking care of the existential needs of the needy, the sick and suffering, the lonely and abandoned, the handicapped and the helpless youths." (Edeh, E.M.P. Peace to the Modern World, 2007, p.2).

It was out of zeal for this his compassionate charism that all his founded Religious Congregations came to be. He founded them to enable him have more hands that can come in contact with all the needy people of God in the world. His experiences of an alternative society while he was overseas for studies challenged him in many ways; he began to ask questions on "why is it that the majority of the people I see here are happy with their lives, enjoy their lives with quality health care," or "Are Nigerians lesser humans?"

It is the combination of all these experiences he had over time and at different places that gave rise to both the man called Fr. Edeh and his philosophy, part of which is to see to the establishment of peace in the world through the provision of medical services and health care especially to those who ordinarily would not be able to afford them and in places where such facilities are usually rare.

At this juncture, we would address ourselves to some of the essential institutions and services established by Fr. Edeh which are health/medical oriented. In doing this, our major concern would be not only to identify the institutions but to highlight what services they provide and above all, to underline how these services are provided.

6. Medical Institutions and Health Care Services of Fr. Edeh

The first health institution established by Fr. Edeh is Our Saviour Hospital / Maternity and Rehabilitation Center in Elele, founded in 1986. This was followed by Our Saviour Motherless Babies Home in Elele in 1992. Then came others in this order: Specialist Diagnostic Laboratory, Enugu (2001), Madonna University Medical Clinic, Okija (2001), Madonna University Teaching Hospital, Elele (2003).

The patients who come to these institutions can be grouped into two groups: The first group consists of those who can pay for their medical treatments and the second group consists of those who are so poor that they can hardly eat not to talk of being able to pay even a penny for their medical treatments. We have many cases of this second group every day. Nevertheless, they are properly treated free of charge under the practical and effective charity of Fr. Edeh's philosophy. Very costly life-saving surgeries have been administered to people of this nature free of charge.

In other words, in these institutions free medications and free surgeries are fully given to those who cannot help themselves in the society. This is a veritable source of giving peace to the world through the mission of practical and effective charity in health care services.

In November 2006, Fr. Edeh organized a programme called Madonna International Charity Peace Award. Part of the objectives, which he realized using this programme, was to extend the same kind of health services in Nigeria to other parts of the world such as Cambodia, Japan, Philippines (Asia). He did this through giving financial awards to victims of natural disasters such as Tsunami, Hurricane and other natural calamities. For this event, many distinguished personalities from various countries were in attendance such as people from the United States of America, Columbia, England, Germany, Poland, Australia, India, and South Africa. This is not to speak of the myriad of imminent Nigerians who participated in the programme.

We strongly believe that the difference which Fr. Edeh has made which he continues to make and which he would make in the area of medical and health care comes more from how the services are rendered than even in simply establishing institutions.

Our Saviour Hospital/Maternity and Rehabilitation Centre is situated within the Elele community where only the abjectly poor individuals are mostly located and this was not simply a chance factor. The location of this health institute was born out of Fr. Edeh's decision and his target was to render selfless and free services with quality health care, with high quality facilities to the local inhabitants. Those found in this area are those who cannot readily afford any payment and therefore are treated and cared for, free of charge. All these have greatly helped in actualizing the philosophy of Fr. Edeh, which is to contribute immensely to peace in the world beginning from Nigeria and precisely with local communities like Elele. One would find that almost his structures and its location are geared towards targeting the population of the less privileged. His intention was to bring health care to the doorsteps of the thousands in the society who cannot help themselves. The same is applicable to many other medical institutions founded by him.

Fr. Edeh does not only have institutions and structures that provide medical services to the needy but has those that form medical personnel who offer the needed services in different places in the world.

7. The Training and Production of Medical Personnel

The Madonna University College of Medicine, School of Nursing, Dentistry, Optometry, Public Health and the Faculty of Pharmaceutical Sciences, all in Elele make up the constituent parts of what we may describe as the factory owned by Fr. Edeh that forms and produces medical personnel. These personnel work in difference places in the world and I happen to be one amongst them. Many others who work in Madonna University Teaching Hospital are resident in the premises and the reason is to give adequate attention to our patients at any given time.

In Madonna University Teaching Hospital, many consultants are assigned to their various specialties to facilitate a quality health care to those who need it and these areas of specializations are:

Department of Internal Medicine: Here the following specialties are readily found, four cardiologists, two neurologists, two rheumatologists, one endocrinologist, one dermatologist, and one nephrologist.

Department of Surgery: Here we have five general surgeons, two pediatric surgeons, and three orthopedic surgeons, and two urologists.

Department of Obstetrics and Gynaecology: It has six obstetricians and gynecologists. Here we care for mostly treatments for women health disorders like infertility, ante-partum/post-partum haemorrhage, ectopic pregnancy, recurrent miscarriages, obstructed labour, fibroids, pre-eclampsia/eclampsia, gestational trophoblastic diseases, menstruation disorders, fistulas, genital prolapse, menopausal disorders, and others

Paediatricians: They are five in number.
Radiologists are two in number.
Radiographers are two in number.
Pathologists are two in number.

There is this saying that a good farmer is one who is known to be ever ready with every required tools and implements whenever he sets out for his business. The same is applicable here in Madonna University Teaching Hospital in the sense that Fr. Edeh, in his magnanimity, made adequate provisions for all the necessary equipment needed in the facilitation of complete medical services and health care. In his zeal to bring good health to the doorpost of every patient that comes his way, he spends fortunes to import latest medical equipment, which is hardly seen in many hospitals in Nigeria, not minding the free cost of treatments.

The following high qualities, minimal to noninvasive latest medical diagnostic equipment are obtainable in Madonna University Teaching Hospital:

a. Modern x-ray machines, which has the lowest possible radiation exposure to patients. With qualified Radiographers and Radiologists.
b. Ultrasound scanning machines, with modern probes and transducers. This is a diagnostic technique in which very high frequency sound wave are passed into the body and the reflected echoes analyzed to build a picture of the internal organs or of a foetus in the uterus. This procedure is painless and considered safe at any time especially during pregnancy.
c. Laparoscopic machines with latest LASER modalities. Laser is an acronym for "Light Amplification by Stimulated Emission of Radiation." LASER cut through tissues without any loss of blood and with minimal scar on the body.

It is one of the newest technologies in medicine which allows some surgeries to be carried out without cutting up a patient and which also minimizes hospital stay and chances of invasion of infections which in some cases leads to wound dehiscence(minimal assess surgery).

d. Endoscopy machine with different probes. This machine enables almost any hollow structure in the body to be viewed and inspected directly without cuts. It is inserted through a natural opening such as the mouth, vagina or into a small incision. It aids the collection of tissues for biopsies.
e. Modern pulse oximeters used in the measurement of blood oxygen levels in the body and many other types of equipments like ventilators and monitors located mostly in the intensive care unit of the hospital.

f. Echocardiograph/ECG machine: This diagnostic technique detects the structural and functional abnormalities of the heart wall, heart chambers, valves, and other congenital heart diseases like aneurysm, pericarditis, cardiomyopathy, etc. (position, functions and size).

In what follows, we intend to see how the structures, facilities, and services provided under Fr. Edeh's medical institutions have responded to the health challenges of the people of Nigeria to the extent that their peace could be associated with the services rendered.

8. Issues of Authenticity and Relevance

In our discussion so far we have been able to underline at different points how beneficial the medical institutions and services provided under the umbrella of Fr. Edeh is to the people of Nigeria and beyond. Nevertheless, we would not like to round off this presentation without focusing a bit further on the issue of authenticity and relevance as it concerns these institutions and services in question. By this, we mean to respond to a simple question: Fr. Edeh established these institutions and services with a view to bringing peace in the world. Is this really happening? Are people experiencing greater peace in their lives, families and communities as a result of the services or healing obtained through these structures of Fr. Edeh?

The way we have chosen to accomplish this task is by establishing how to a large extent good health of mind and body is essentially related to peace, not only of the individual persons but also of a community and a nation as a whole.

9. Good Health and Peace of Mind

There is a famous adage, which says that a healthy mind dwells in a healthy body and good health is wealth. As we know, a healthy mind is vital for peace.

What is good health? It is simply the absence of physical and mental disease with regular exercise. But according to the World Health Organization definition of health, "it is a state of complete physical, mental and social well-being and not merely the absence of disease or infirmity" (adopted by the International Health Conference, New York, 19-22 June 1946). To achieve a good health, all people should have the opportunity to fulfill their genetic potentials. This includes the ability to develop without the impediments of poor nutrition, environmental contamination, or infectious diseases. Good health is key to happiness because a healthy body is a healthy mind.

What is peace? Peace is not simply the absence of war or fighting, or an agreement to end a war. It refers to a state of general completeness or well-being, harmony. It means to be sound, to be safe, wholeness, total health. In scripture, the most appropriate word for peace is shalom.

For the sake of peace, we must destroy our arsenal of rational nuclear weapons, including condemning, belittling, comparing, labelling, insulting, sarcastic, and condescending. Let us chose to do everything possible on our own part to live in peace with one another. A paraphrase of Jesus' seventh beatitude says, "You are blessed when you can show people how to cooperate instead of compete and fight."

It is unrealistic to expect everyone to agree about everything, yet we can re-establish a relationship even when we are unable to resolve our differences. Christians often have legitimate honest disagreements and differing opinions, but we can disagree without being disagreeable. The same diamond looks differently from different angles. God expects unity, not uniformity, and we can walk arminarm without seeing eye to eye on every issue because as Warren rightly observes,

"Reconciliation focuses on the relationship while resolution focuses on the problem. When we focus on reconciliation, the problem loses significance and often becomes irrelevant".

As St Paul puts it, the kingdom of God is all about peace; the kingdom and Jesus central message is all about peace.

Now, the point we wish to establish is that since the central message of Jesus Christ is about the kingdom of God, and peace is at the heart of the kingdom of God, then Fr. Edeh's medical and health services which are derived from his philosophy and are geared towards peace in the world can logically be said to be an authentic continuation of the life and ministry of Jesus Christ in the world today.

Conclusion

So far, we have examined Fr. Edeh's medical institutions and services and their contributions to world peace. Placing these services and care in the context of Nigeria where good medical treatment is not within the reach of the average citizen we left nobody in doubt about the relevance and significance of these noble foundations of Fr. Edeh. Thinking about how early these establishments are, we conclude that his philosophy of world peace through health care and services is almost as old as the man called Fr. Edeh. The beneficiaries of these services are innumerable and the ultimate result of what they receive through Fr. Edeh is peace. For when any member of the family is sick, there is no peace in the family and when health is restored, peace returns. Therefore, the claim that Fr. Edeh is contributing significantly to world peace through medical services and health care has an absolute merit. It is not just something to be believed but to be accepted because there are facts to support it. Finally, this philosophy and the actions born from it deserve support, appreciation, and continuity. Permit me, therefore, to conclude by saying that the whole world should appreciate profoundly all that Fr. Edeh has done, is doing and will still do in the area of medical institutions and services towards achieving peace in the whole world. The works and achievements of Fr. Edeh will certainly continue forever, for the institutions and the services are established with the assurance of continuity guaranteed through Fr. Edeh's foundation of four religious congregations whose charism and apostolate constitute the perpetual excursion and continuation of Fr. Edeh's mission of practical and effective charity geared towards the realization of peace to millions in the modern world. With life and people like Fr. Edeh, there is no doubt that the realization of world peace will one day be actualized. To God be praised for his life, his philosophy and his activities. In the following chapter, we shall examine the impact of Edehism on Girl-Child care and education.

CHAPTER THREE

IMPACT OF EDEHISM ON THE DEVELOPMENT OF GIRL-CHILD EDUCATION

By Dr. Regina Acholonu

Abstract

Thinking of world peace without gender equality in education is a mirage. Hence Prof. Edeh has shown through his numerous educational institutions great support of women education and empowerment gearing towards their emancipation and peace in the world.

Introduction

Over the years, the education of the Girl-Child in Africa has attracted global attention. Discrimination on the basis of sex is prevalent in most societies and often starts at the earliest stages of life. A girl's worth and status is considered to be lower than that of a boy and therefore the Girl-Child is devalued. Some girls are barred from acquiring formal education and in a situation where they are allowed to attend school, a good number of them are later withdrawn for one reason or the other. The starting point is the prevalent traditional practice of son preference. This is directly traceable to the patrilineal system of inheritance by males. The Girl-Child is regarded as a bad investment because she would marry outside the family. Consequently, less emphasis is placed on girls' education.

Gender bias is the outcome of a complex combination of cultural and societal attitudes, traditional beliefs and practices based on patriarchy and other aggravated economic circumstances. In many societies, sons carry on the lineage and the family name; perform funeral or burial rites for parents and religious rituals for ancestors. Daughters are viewed as transient, to be given away in marriage. Her productivity if any and fertility would only benefit her husband and his family.

Traditionally, the Girl-Child is disadvantaged from birth. Families make conscious or unconscious decisions on intra-family resource allocations. In the context of scarcity, they allocate their limited resources in a way that will give the best returns to sons. The daughters are discriminated against in access to food, clothing, health care and education.

The Girl-Child is vulnerable to sexual exploitation within the family and commercially. Incest and other forms of sexual exploitation of the Girl-Child by family members go unnoticed and unpunished because these are covered up by the family.

Increasing urbanization, loss of traditional means of livelihood, loss of extended family support, the social evils of urban slums and growing tourism have contributed to widespread trafficking in children and Girl-Child prostitution. The Girl-Child is often forced into prostitution under debt-bondage. The minor girls are forced to work under exploitative, coercive, and unhygienic conditions without access to health care or protection against sexually communicable diseases (Tomaszewski, 1993).

Concept of Girl-Child Education

Education all over the world and at every time in history is seen as a process of bringing desirable change into the behaviour of human beings (Dahama & Bhatnager, 2005). Plato, one of the leading Greek educators in his classic the Republic, maintains that any effective education must provide justice, morality and righteousness (Obidi, 1993). Another great Greek educator, Aristotle, holds tenaciously that the aim of education is to produce man and woman who have the right kind of intelligence and ability as well as the right type of character (Obidi, 1993). Jean Jacques Rousseau, a leading French educator, emphasizes that education should inculcate in the child virtues of morality.

Many other educators and stakeholders in education are consistent on the notion that meaningful education begins with the child and has morality as its basic component. Education therefore is a means of acquiring knowledge, learning and training of some sort. It is a means by which the child receives orientation about a subject over a period of time at school or an institution of higher learning. It is the process through which a child is taught better ways of doing things or a better way of living. Eyibe (2006), in his reasoning notes that, to qualify as an educated person, the individual must have acquired the following five basic functional skills in order of priority: behavioural skills, intellectual skills, writing skills, technical/ technological skills and speaking skills.

The reason behind educational institution establishment is for the acquisition of general knowledge or technical skills that will enable the child to make the best out of life.

Technical knowledge aims at imparting artistic skills and method of technical applications, which are different in various disciplines.

Education is perhaps the strongest variable affecting the status of the Girl-Child yet education of the Girl-Child is often neglected. Research findings have shown that investing on educating girls is the best possible investment for development. But there are so many barriers to Girl-Child education, especially in Africa. Wide gender gaps persist at all levels of education including the most basic level that is the primary school enrolment. To understand why fewer girls than boys enroll in schools and more girls than boys drop out of school, one has to consider a complex web of cultural, social and economic factors that affect the education of boys and girls differently.

Cultures and Traditions that Perpetuate Gender Differences in Education:

i.   The belief that sons look after their parents in their old age, while daughters marry out of their own families at a young age and join their husbands' families is one of the cultural factors that are held rigidly on to in Africa. Sons are valued for their anticipated financial contributions to the household whereas the daughters' economic contribution if at all any would benefit their husbands' family.

ii. Prevalence of son preference and certain other traditional beliefs and practices result in neglect of girls in terms of health care, and nutrition.

iii. When a society practices seclusion of women, girls may only attend sex-segregated schools. This means that girls' access to education depends on the availability of single sex schools.

iv. Direct Costs and Opportunity Costs of Educating Girls

Poverty also has enormous impact on girls' chances of schooling. Such households allocate their limited resources to the education of sons because it is believed that this would bring larger benefits to the household in terms of future income. In rural households in particular, Girl-Child labour is essential for the maintenance of the household. Like adult women, they perform economic activities as well as performing household works like cooking, cleaning the home, fetching water and taking care of the younger siblings.

v. Availability of Female Teachers

This can also determine the Girl-Child enrolment at school. Many parents in traditional societies are more willing to send their daughters to school if there are women teachers. But the problem still remains that there are usually very few female teachers in most of these regions.

vi. The curricular is not really relevant considering the potential role of girls as mothers and housewives in rural areas

Uneducated parents are usually unaware of the benefits of educating girls in terms of current health and welfare of the family and in terms of its inter-generational effects. An improved educational level among parents has a positive impact on girl's education.

vii. Early Child Marriage

Early marriage has serious implications for the Girl-Child including health hazards, the end of schooling, limited economic opportunities, disruption of personal development and often early divorce. Divorced girls are legally seen as adults and are vulnerable to trafficking as a result of the economic vulnerability.

Functions of Girl-Child Education

According to a World Bank statement (1989), women's education is the "most influential single investment that can be made in the developing world." Many governments and individuals now support women's education not only to foster economic growth but also to promote smaller families, increase and improve child health. Educating women is an important end in itself.

Educated Women are Concerned with Family Planning

Women with more schooling tend to have smaller, healthier families. Throughout the world, more education is associated with smaller family size. In most less developed countries, women with no education have about twice the number of children as women with ten or more years in school. Women with more education usually make a later, adult transition into adulthood. They marry later, want smaller families and are likely to make such decisions of having only the number of children they can conveniently cater for.

The Concept of Edehism

We are aware of the philosophic systems of great philosophers like Socrates, Plato, Aristotle, Thomas Aquinas, etc. Today we are witnessing to the system of Thought and Action of Emmanuel Edeh, known as Edehism. Edehism, as one of the 'isms' in philosophy, is a practical theory of metaphysics which is quite distinct from the Western and Oriental philosophies of Socratism, Platonism, Aristotleanism, Shoitism, Confucianism, Taoism, and so on (Onyewuenyi, 2011). Edehism is a system of thought and action. Emmanuel Edeh's philosophy is all-encompassing. It aims at the comprehension of a whole mode of life. Its search for meanings and for life in its various expressions singles out Edeh's philosophy. (Onyewuenyi, 2011) We will now focus on some of the key philosophical concepts that inform his philosophy of practical and effective charity.

Being "Good That Is"

For Edeh, a being is the good that is, which embraces all existence starting from the supreme being (*Chukwu*) to the least existent being. It is an echo of scholastic philosophy of *ens est bonum*. God is the highest good (*Chiamaka*) the maximum good (*Chi-bu-mma*). He is the source of goodness and what he created is good. Humans participate in this goodness.

The Igbo metaphysics, in the main, asserts man as *mma di*, that is the "good that is." The Edehistic man as "good that is" is based on man having been created by God the Supreme Being, *Chineke, Osebuluwa* as God Almighty who is the source of goodness. It maintains that man's life, existence and values, such as goodness and peace are fundamentally sourced from the *Chineke* the Omnipotent God, the ultimate being who is responsible for goodness. The Edehistic metaphysics treasures man by considering him holistically with regards to his spiritual, socio-economic aspirations. It does not perceive man as some psychologists, sociologists, psychoanalysts, cultural anthropologists, Western philosophers, scientists, and economists do (Onyewuenyi, 2011).

Concept of Development

Development is one concept which has over the years attracted global attention. It pays attention to questions bordering on poverty, unemployment and inequality (Seers, 1969). It is a multi-dimensional process, which involves quantitative and qualitative changes in structures and institutions of a society. Todaro (1981), states that development is a process of improving the quality of all human lives in a society. In his submission, Ake (1996) states that development is a process by which people create and recreate themselves and their circumstances to realize higher levels of civilizations in accordance with their own choices and value. This, Idode (1989) further suggests could only occur when individuals and societies confront their problems and attempt to solve them and become able to control their environment.

Odekunle, in his contributions (2008), sees development as the continuous improvement in the quality of life and existence, which improvement is increasingly and evenly distributed among the overwhelming majority of the population. In addition, there is necessarily the element of sustainability whereby the continuity in the improvement and its increasingly even distribution can be maintained, upheld, nourished over an appreciable period of time.

Theoretical Framework

This research finds expression in the social responsibility theory. In this case, the social responsibility theory hinges on the social responsibility roles of one man, Fr. Edeh. Some of the assumptions of the social responsibility as is described by Dominick (2002) are that the individual has a responsibility to preserve democracy and respond to society's needs and interests.

EPTAISM as a philosophy provides an avenue for the exchange of comments and criticism. This theory is apt in the sense that Edeh being a great philosopher has done so much in responding positively to the needs and interests of the society through his numerous educational institutions and other vocational outfits. He also owns attached to his universities, broadcast media, which provide avenues for the exchange of comments and criticisms.

Edeh's Philosophy of Practical and Effective Doing (Charity) and Girl-Child Education

Fair treatment, justice and freedom are not just desired by all humans but are fundamental to human existence, the world over. Issues of social interaction and wellbeing, equality, fairness, and rights are critical to human survival. It needs to be emphasized that the wheel of development is lubricated by our understanding of these indispensable variables, equity and human rights.

Equity is a word, which has many meanings. For instance, it simply refers to that which is fair, just, moral and ethical (Oxford Advanced Learner's Dictionary, 2005). In a legal sense, equity is the set of rules first fashioned out and administered by the court of Chancery in England. Here one does not intend to explore equity in its strictest legal sense but rather more of its literal sense to suit its application in the context of the issue in question. In essence, maintaining equity in social activities brings about efficient human relations. The principles of equity and justice form the basis for equity jurisdiction.

Justice is a concept that is widely used in many spheres of human life. It is present in the conscience of men and it is simply translated as equitableness

(Udiugwomen, 2005).Generally, equity and human rights are essential to the survival of any nation as they are the foundations of peace among men. Human rights are those rights, which the international community recognizes as belonging to all individuals by the very fact of their humanity.

Fr. Edeh is among the few individuals in our world today who critically believes and acts in accordance with the tenets of equity, justice and human rights. He has successfully expunged the harsh conditions meted against the Girl-Child in the name of culture. Consequently he has given hope and succour to the Girl-Child who otherwise would have become a liability or a deviant in the society. His most powerful weapon in combating these inhuman conditions against the Girl-Child is his philosophy of *mmadi*; the philosophy of practical and effective charity; the good that is, being that manifests itself in action.

With this philosophy of *mmadi*, he has penetrated deeply into the fabrics of many lives. He has shown great dynamism in curbing the social ills against the Girl-Child education and has successfully created great awareness that Girl-Child education is indeed the most influential single investment that can be made in a developing world like Nigeria.

Through his Philosophy of Thought and Action, he has achieved so much in the educational empowerment of the Girl-Child both nationally and internationally.

The Congregation of Sisters of Jesus the Saviour was founded by Edeh at Elele in 1984. This institution was founded to fulfill the spiritual yearnings of young girls who have vowed to remain chaste, poor and obedient to the greater glory of God. A congregation that had an initial intake of twenty-six young girls has spread to all the nooks and cranny of Nigeria and the international world. Many of the sisters are studying in universities and institutions of higher learning in Nigeria and overseas while many more others are on mission works in countries like St. Lucia in West Indies, Netturno in Central Rome, Detroit in the USA, Nigeria in Africa, etc. doing various kinds of vocational charity works like giving shelter, clothing, and feeding the helpless and running old peoples' homes for the aged. The sisters have established a project called Centre for the Poor. Here they care for the abjectly impoverished members of the Nigerian society, the handicapped and the sick. The inmates of this centre come from different parts of Nigeria.

Apart from the Spiritual Vocational institutions and in the words of Onyewuenyi (2012), Edeh has put into action several youth empowerment programmes, which aim at addressing the oppression, stratification and inequality found among Girl-Child Girl-Children. Youth empowerment also focuses at providing Girl-Child Girl-Children with the opportunities and means to genuinely serve others in society and grow into confident leaders.

Such Girl-Child empowerment programmes include the Youth Rehabilitation Centre established in 1986 at Elele to cater for thousands of jobless youths. Here they are empowered to become self reliant in various fields of endeavour that will in the end earn them a living in life.

Scholarship programmes for the handicapped are as follows:

Free education is offered to indigent youths in the society regardless of their creed and ethnicity. These indigent students are found in all Edeh's universities and institutions of higher learning. Through his numerous educational institutions, he has contributed and is still contributing immensely to Girl-Child education. In Edeh's philosophy of practical and effective charity, there is no distinction between man and woman, girl and boy. There is no preferential treatment on the basis of gender. Admissions into all his educational institutions are open to both boys and girls. Edeh's consideration for women in the area of employment is worth mentioning. In his entire establishments, women have equal employment opportunity with men as opposed to what is obtainable in the society. This goes a long way in encouraging parents to see every need to invest in Girl-Child education.

Conclusion

The realization that, without the attainment of gender equality, the millennium development goals will not be achieved should heighten the need to progressively monitor efforts with regards to Girl-Child education. To this end therefore, the very few individuals in the society who through their social responsibility roles have given priority to girl child education should be highly commended.

Edeh through his numerous educational institutions has highlighted the potentials and capabilities of the Girl-Child. Nigeria is a multi-cultural nation of diverse people, multiple identities and colourful outlook. It has a population of 150 million and 400 ethnic groups. Government alone cannot achieve the qualitative education that would give every Nigerian child, girl or boy, the opportunity to aspire in education.

In fact, no federal or state government alone can fund qualitative education especially with their lack of firm attitudes towards the provision of qualitative education. The society should therefore appreciate the efforts of this great man Rev. Fr. Prof. Emmanuel Edeh who has done so much in establishing for both girls and boys qualitative educational institutions with excellent moral values at the barest minimum costs for the parents. How many governments can attempt what he has achieved? He deserves unparalleled recognition.

CHAPTER FOUR

EDUCATION AND WOMEN EMPOWERMENT IN EDEH'S PRACTICAL PHILOSOPHY; IMPLICATIONS FOR GLOBAL PEACE

By Sr. Purissima Egbepkalu SJS Ph.D

Abstract

Peace is at the root of every man's craving. But ironically, the more man desires peace, the more he finds himself in a state of discord, war and helplessness. A lot has been done both at personal and communal levels to ensure peace but each time, it seems nothing works out for good. Many homes, communities, nations are in turmoil and desirous of peace to live as humans they are. Unfortunately, they are cut in the web of despair because they nurse the feeling that peace is still far from them. Touched by this situation, the contemporary African philosopher, Edeh Emmanuel proffered a pragmatic and lasting solution for realization of genuine peace. With his philosophical articulations on the profound being of man from an African metaphysical perspective, he presented to the world a logical scheme of a concrete and an authentic existence for the attainment of true peace and its sustainability that is also valid for all nations, colour, race, language and religion. His argument on the possibility of the universal validity of his practical thought reveals that all created men have a common ontological nature having emanated from the same creative source. As good-natured beings therefore, men actualize and preserve the essence of their being through collective responsibility of brotherly care, love and respect for one another, which has consequential effect of true peaceful convivum radiating from personal to communal and of course to the world at large creating a global peaceful existence. Therefore, the understanding that each person deserves respect, care and love and adhering to it in concrete daily activities in an uninterrupted spin that begins from each single individual and spreads throughout the globe proves a logical and pragmatic tool for lasting global peace. In Edeh's practical-peace scheme, the use and more production of arms and ammunition are set aside as they encourage further discord and war. This research evaluates Edeh's philosophical peace model as it is anchored in the ontology of man as "mmadi" (good that is) and a peaceful creature who naturally seeks to live in accordance to his good nature for the realization of his profound being. It also addresses a few challenges that militate against man's natural and peaceful existence and the factors that can promote it which include education and good character formation. Education we all know is a very powerful tool for both human and societal developments. Meanwhile, education that is limited to only a particular gender, that of male, which reflects virtually in all cultures especially in developing countries, can only guarantee partial realization of peace both at personal and global levels. Just as a saying goes that, "A state that does not educate and train women is like a man who only trains his right arm." Therefore, educating and empowering women becomes imperative for the actualization and sustenance of global peace.

Introduction

A great African patriot, Nelson Mandela once said, "Education is the most powerful weapon which you can use to change the world." With his practical philosophy, Fr. Edeh remains one of the greatest personalities that have changed the world reasonably with particular reference to our great nation Nigeria through education by which he empowers the youths, women included. His educational institutions practically implemented at all levels operate on two strong pillars of academic and moral excellence taking into cognizance that good education without good morals can be ruinous. As a jinx breaker, he ventured into private tertiary education and proved to the world that good education of both men and women equips them with the power to think clearly, offers them the opportunity to appreciate their lives and that of others as goods that are, helps them to develop better in respect of human dignity, and challenges them to contribute constructively to the growth of their nations and the world at large.

This research will expose our philosopher's practical thought as it relates to education and empowerment of women in human and national development for the realization of global peace. It will first depict generally his philosophical perspective as a peace model and as a precursor of the United Nations Millennium Development Goals because of its practical emphasis on the realities of life mirrored in the UN goals. His philosophy of education as a catalyst for constructive development and also in great favour of women empowerment will also be evaluated with regard to its efficacy as a veritable tool for the actualization of gender equality and consequently the realization of human dignity and promotion of peace. The drama of Edeh's pragmatic philosophical logic will therefore be presented as enhancing and sustaining a global peace, the impossible project that proves itself possible through the harmonization of thought and action in accordance with the nature of man who true to his nature as *homo-cura* in an incessant spin of brotherly love, care and respect one another; the loving exercise that begins with every single individual.

Edeh's Philosophy: A Peace Model

Fr. Prof. Edeh's publication of his classical work *Towards an Igbo Metaphysics* in 1985 positively influenced the course of history and people's thought pattern especially with regard to who man is, the profundity of his being, his purpose in life and his destiny, etc. His ingenuity to unravel the mystery of man, analyzing him ontologically as the *mmadi* (good that is) expresses an existential approach that touches the core of man's raison d'être. Hence, the understanding of what it means to philosophize continues to manifest itself more strongly in practical matters of people's concrete experiences of their daily lives particularly in African setting. It becomes then obvious that "the question regarding the Being (Reason) of beings received also a convincing explication that is easy to understand even by a non-philosopher and non-African philosopher." (Purissima, E., 2011, p.7). This invaluable philosophical contribution has greatly availed man the opportunity of coming closer to his humanity, which is a grand trail to personal and communal peace.

Edeh's notion of man as *mmadi* gives an incontrovertible understanding that veritably conforming to the truth of reality of his ontology, man can only express that which is ontological of him; being true to his nature since one can only give what one has. That means, since he is a good that is, he cannot not exist and continue to actualize his good nature, which greatly implies living peacefully. According to him, "to be is to be the good

41

that is." (Edeh, E.M.P., 2007, p.145). However, one recognizes swiftly the resultant effect of his assertion of man's natural goodness as the collective existential responsibility of caring which by implication endows each man with an inherent virtue of caring and renders each man *homo-cura* (a caring man). The caring that Edeh emphasizes embraces all ramifications of life because man is an integral being whose wholeness is realized in the complementarity and interplay of the physical and spiritual dimensions.

Having noted that living true to his nature makes man exist authentically, we delineate that at the root of the responsibility of caring is the spirit of true and sincere brotherliness and respect for one another having emanated from one and the same creative source as the beauty of life and live in the same world designed by the same supreme being. As it is clearly stated, "The above metaphysical and existential implication of man's nature as the good that is portrays a very serious ontological quality of human relations as members from the same descendants. The true African notion of man that Edeh's philosophical anthropology captures, clarifies at the same time the intention of the founding fathers of African society that has at its base respect and care for life for it is sacred" (Purissima, E., 2011, p.5).By implication therefore, man's true existence should be a peaceful one that promotes human dignity. Edeh's philosophy so understood is no doubt said to be a peace model of existential and pragmatic thought.

Edeh's Pragmatic Philosophy: A Precursor of the United Nations Millennium Development Goals (MDGs)

Edeh's philosophical convictions do not allow him to limit his philosophical activities to mere rationality because that may be a continuous eruption of human nature. Instead he applied his philosophical maxims; that man is good and deserves care to practical life' existence postulating that,

> If we accept man as the good that is, we must establish realities that depict man as such, realities that are metaphysically focused towards uplifting man from his low state that tends to make man sub-human,that is, the state that categorizes him as the sick, the suffering, the abjectly poor, the handicapped, the deaf, the dumb, the blind, the abandoned, the crippled, the helpless, the uneducated, etc. (Edeh, E.M.P., 2007, pp.5ff).

His undaunted and compassionate care encompasses all aspects of man's life. His innovation in educational sector for which we are here directly concerned is a pragmatic and eloquent testimony of an intermingling of a meaningful philosophical endeavour and life of care in accordance to the ontological nature of man. "For what is the usefulness of our thought if not to aid man realize the fullness of his being and live peacefully?" he would ask. The prompting to respond to the dire need of people especially the Africans, he considered as very urgent and without any least of doubt, it harbours the lines of United Nations' declaration of MDGs and even more. For this very reason, I consider his practical philosophical contribution as a forerunner of MDGs. That is to say, that even before the United Nations declared in the year 2000 eight major goals to be achieved by its member states by 2015, Edeh has underscored their optimal importance especially goals one, two, three four, five, and six which have to do with eradicating extreme poverty and hunger, achieving universal primary education, promoting gender equality and empowering women, reducing child mortality, improving maternal health, combating HIV/AIDS and other diseases respectively as veritable tools to uphold human dignity, accelerate development and ensure its sustainability as well as the realization of global peace. Beyond the above listed goals, he is equally committed through his rehabilitation scheme to the revitalization, restoration of hope, ensuring peace and giving new lease of life to those who have fallen victims of our depressed society: the down trodden, the hopeless, the sick especially those that are psychologically, emotional, economically, and spiritually affected. His philosophical conviction also spurred him into protecting the minority and the vulnerable groups, which include the children, women, the handicapped, and the less privileged.

Education in Edeh: A Catalyst for Constructive Development

Education we all know is always linked to development as it is a vital tool for personal, national and global developments and their sustainability. Education simply defined is "the process of teaching and learning, usually at school, college or university" (Longman Dictionary, 2007). This implies that an educated person is one who has been well taught and who has learnt a lot.

However, the above definition seems insufficient for the purpose of this research. I will therefore employ the philosophers' understanding of education to serve the purpose of this presentation. The philosophers we all know are regarded as those who love and pursue wisdom and knowledge, while philosophy remains the seat of all knowledge. For them, education is not just the art of imparting and acquiring knowledge but also that of habit. The ultimate end and value of education may be summarized as the realization of famous Latin quotation *Mens sana in corpore sano*, often translated as "a sound mind in a healthy body" attributed to the pre-Socratic philosopher, Thales but also well adopted by John Locke, a philosopher who committed so much to education and whose educational thought pattern influenced American education.

While Socrates believed that knowledge is virtue and ignorance vice, Aristotle who imagined that "the educated differ from the uneducated as much as the living differ from the dead," held the opinion that proper education should be based on three basic principles: the golden mean, the possible and the becoming (cf. Sharma, P., 2008, p.2). According to him, in corresponding to the gradual unfolding of mental and physical abilities of man, education should have the core concern of preserving the citizen and ensuring his peace and happiness by training him in virtues which is the perfection of human reason; reason being the first source of knowledge and active reasons make the world intelligible (cf. Mays, E., edited 2011).As the contemporary Aristotle, Edeh's concept of education greatly coincides with his ontological understanding of man. Though the basic aim of education has not changed but the art of educating a contemporary man has drifted a little in order to meet up with the challenges of the time. Therefore, the response of our contemporary philosopher, Edeh as to what a proper education should be especially the education of the youth of our time is practically seen in his educational structures which promote knowledge as it relates to a healthy lifestyle that informs his institutional motto—*Dignitas Scientiae et Moralis* (excellence in education and morals). True to this motto, he has lifted education to a pride of place in our nation. His breakthrough in educational sphere from the cradle to tertiary level has really contributed to the positive development of the citizens especially the youth. Infact, at tertiary level, he was a jinx breaker, a role model in restoring the dignity of education in the country where moral decadence has eaten deep into the life of the people—especially the youth and women—who are not just the future and hope of our nation but today's major stakeholders for development of our nation and the world at large. He has maintained his policy of high standard in character and learning in all his institutions, knowing full well that education without good morals is more dangerous and suicidal. In other words, the true goal of education is the harmony of intelligence and good character. Otherwise it will result to education without values, which as useful as it may be, seems rather to make man a cleverer devil."

Education is a dynamic process with an integral formation and approach that portrays knowledge, character and behaviour dimensions. It aims at discerning the truth about reality and integrating such truth in concrete phenomena of life. The educand is not a vessel to be filled up but he is like a candle to be enkindled in which case his personality naturally, harmoniously, and progressively unfolds itself; his potentials, interests, motivations, beliefs, ideals, habits, powers, visions, and horizon enlarges according to his natural endowment so that he becomes the best he can in knowledge and character.

True development for both the individual and the nation therefore lies in the true and honest actualization of one's abilities for an authentic, happy and peaceful existence. Edeh's concept of education can be likened to that of Plato. In his famous Republic, Plato asserts that each citizen must be trained according to his capacity to understand and unfold his abilities for his personal and social wellbeing. In fact, his understanding of justice lies in the fact that an individual should be disposed to acquire relevant skills that he can and then practice that which he is naturally best fit for. According to him, "Do not train children to learning by force and harshness, but direct them to it by what amuses their minds, so that you may be better able to discover with accuracy the peculiar bent of the genius of each." For Leonard da Vinci would add, "Study without desire spoils the memory, and it retains nothing that it takes in." The search for knowledge seeks to understand oneself for self-realization of one's nature. In this way, a healthy mind in a healthy body is achieved. But inappropriate unfolding and mismanagement of the individual's nature leads to personal crises, social ills, unhappiness, etc.

Edeh's Educational Structure: Pathway to realization of Human Dignity, Empowering and Protecting Women

Empowering women falls in line with Edeh's philosophical convictions:

As goods that are women need to be cared for and nurtured. One must respect and uphold their human dignity. They need to be educated and introduced properly into the wider world. To enhance their understanding of the society in order to contribute to its development because one does better only when one knows better, women need to expand their horizon for decision making, to be gainfully and happily employed, to sentence hunger, violence, abuse, etc. and be encouraged to live fulfilled and peaceful life.

Brigham Young once remarked that when you "educate a boy, you educate an individual. Educate a girl, and you educate a community". This may reveal that women have natural tendency and vocation to love and live by heart, which is the seat of feeling, care and kindness required to bind the human community in peace and with their resilient ability, to stay on in patience, despite all odds, great difficulties and tensions. Besides, they transmit faster and more profoundly their wealth of knowledge and good morals to the next generation because they are the primary companions and teachers of their children, being closest to them in strong relational loving bond. In the words of Benedict XVI, "The joyful love with which our parents welcomed us and accompanied our first steps in this world is like a sacramental sign and prolongation of the benevolent love of God from which we have come. The experience of being welcomed and loved by God and by our parents is always the firm foundation for authentic human growth and authentic development, helping us to mature on the way towards truth and love and to move beyond ourselves in order to enter into communion with others and with God." (Benedict XVI, July 2006).

For the above facts among others, it is important to delineate that Edeh does not only empower women, he also protects them against all forms of violence and abuses; physical, emotional, psychological, etc. that militate against their development and realization of peace. For example, his educational structure defies all forms of sexual abuse against both men and women such as secret cultism, strike actions, examination malpractices, etc. Edeh's educational idea structured on decency in education and moral is a sure pathway and safeguard to global peace because to educate a person only in mind and not in character is a risk to the society and menace to human dignity. Sound mind with sound behaviour is a better safeguard of liberty than a standing army.

Education and Women Empowerment in Edeh: Effective Tools for Actualization of Gender Equality and Promotion of Peace

It has been emphasized that knowledge of truth and personal abilities are powerful tools for fulfilled engagement, happiness and peace. "Knowledge is power." Empowerment is usually used in connection with the liberation of the female folk from the patriarchal mentality of the existing culture that seem to marginalize them. It means enablement and it "refers broadly to the expansion of freedoms including those of choice and action to shape one's life" (Narayan, D., 2005, p.4). This implies that they are availed the opportunity to control and manage their lives educationally, economically, politically and participate fully in the development of the society. Education has proved itself a great equalizer of human conditions. However, it is important to note that in as much as fair treatment of all is of paramount important as it promotes social justice and peace, "gender equality does not remove the traditional roles bestowed on each sex neither does it mean that men and women are equal. It rather means that the rights, opportunities and responsibilities of individuals are not based on sex" (Anumudu M.U., & Ononuju N.A., April 2011).From Edeh's philosophy of being, it becomes obvious that men and women are equally created and gifted for the growth of the society. Therefore, any attempt to undermine such natural structure will have consequential effects of disharmony and disequilibrium. To this effect, the 1979 Convention on the Elimination of All Forms of Discrimination against Women adopted by United Nations General Assembly declared the rights, freedom, and equality of women under law. Besides, Pope John Paul II in his Apostolic Letter *Mulieris Dignitatem: On the Dignity and Vocation of Women on the occasion of Marian Year* submits that human dignity commands that members of the society—man and woman alike—be allowed to take part in the decisions that affect them in the climate of genuine freedom (cf. John Paul II, 15 August, 1988). To emphasize the importance of this, the UN Assembly later in 2000 incorporated the need for gender equality in the Millennium Goals to be achieved by 2015. So understood, the grandeur of sex differentiation demands that each of the genders be accorded the respect due to him or her as they complement each other to attain unity in their diversity in responding to the social roles and automatic divisions of labour in the family generated by these enormous physiological differences. Against this background, I found the famous women's slogan "What a man can do, a woman can do it also even better" as an inspiration to compete with men and gives a ready-to-fight impression which their very nature abhors. At this point, "it becomes necessary to delineate that equality does not mean sameness or exhibiting exact responsibilities. Men are gifted with masculine nature, while women on the other hand are also naturally equipped but with feminine body and soul that account for their extraordinary qualities for motherhood." (Purissima, E., 17 December 2011). They combine this unique purpose and capacity with their roles within and outside the family in a manner that makes them uniquely different from men (John Paul II, *op. cit.*).

Edeh's understanding of man and the consequential responsibility of keeping and maintaining peace do not discriminate one gender against the other. How can there be peace when certain people suffer from:

· Marginalization,
· Not considered in decision making,
· Deprivation of right to properties,
· Unpreferred (Girl-Child),
· Unfair treatment,
· Social relegation,
· Violence—physical, emotional, psychological, and so on?

His philosophical position encourages social justice as a veritable avenue to true global peace. Education has a great potential in transforming the society. He recognizes that women are forces to reckon with in the society because of their disposition to service in unity and love and are indispensably required in rendering humane leadership services. In fact, just as creation was not complete without a woman, peace will not be achieved without a woman's full participation in the society. One can rightly affirm that the roles of women remain conspicuous in God's eternal master plan for natural order. The great philosopher Pope John Paul II enlightens that, "Motherhood shows a creativity on which the humanity of each human being largely depends; it also invites man to learn and to express his own fatherhood. Thus women contribute to society and to the Church their ability to nurture human beings." (John Paul II).

Global Peace as an Impossible-Possible Project: Edeh's Pragmatic Philosophical Logic

Peace, a seemingly impossible project becomes naturally possible in Edeh's pragmatic peace-scheme. His philosophy of being from African point of view demonstrates that "the African principle of being one's brother's keeper is not simply a remnant of tribal society". (Edeh, E.M.P., 2007, p.154).It also "offers other peoples an ideal of human existence, especially an ideal of human dignity based upon the belief that all beings created by God are ontologically good and deserve respect...the attentive mind will discern in it a reflection of God-man-world scheme. (ibid, p.154)

The understanding of man a good that is, is a practical key to individual peace that results in global peace with education as an effective tool to live a meaningful and fulfilled life as well as to contribute to the general development of the society. Therefore, he advocates that everyone, young and old, men and women be given equal opportunity and access to education. "For this convincing fact, Fr. Edeh remains optimistic that man can achieve peace in so far as he lives according to his true nature, despite the complexity of life's phenomena that has lured many into developing pessimistic view of life..." (Purissima, E., 2011, p.5ff). Hence, "Edeh continues to invite all of us to the practical uplift of the good in man and the beauty of his creation for a true global peaceful living, genuine and lasting peace cannot be achieved except through a proper perception of man and his real nature as the good that is, and live in accordance to it in the humane human community, where everybody is surrounded with love and fraternal care closed-ness and extreme individualism that can easily arouse resentments and grievances of loneliness in man." (*loc. cit.*).In his logical thought, "Love and charity become therefore the binding forces that hold the human community together and have the characters of relinquishing the evil thoughts and acts from the hearts of men as everyone is his brother's true keeper"(*loc. cit*).

Edeh's peace-scheme can be summarized thus, to live is to love, to attain genuine and enduring global peace is to properly perceive man and his real nature as the good that is and live in accordance to it through relatedness in the humane human community surrounded with love and fraternal care. His philosophical logic of brotherly love is hereby depicted:

Edeh's Pragmatic Logic: An Existential Approach
Self-understanding (as a good that is)
Understanding of others (as same goods that are)
Interpersonal understanding of selves (sacred beings)
Global peace (live and aid others to live)

GLOBAL PEACE

MGs +SGs + CCS + LAL
Love, care, and respect
Peaceful convivum

Recommendations

At this juncture, we hereby recommend that:

· Re-orientation of the masses
· Peace education for all
· Healing exercises
· Starting afresh and
· Philosophers should live up to their professional roles

Conclusion

Peace, a seemingly impossible project becomes naturally possible, thanks to Edeh's philosophical elucidations; the understanding that all men are good natured and peaceful beings who actualize and preserve the essence of their beings through collective responsibility of brotherly care, love and respect for one another which has consequential effect of true peaceful convivum. According to him, this assertion is valid for all nations, colour, race, language and religion, having emanated from the same creative source. Also, just as the Bible reveals that creation was not complete without the presence of a woman, so also the world suffers because of the marginalization of women which creates a missing link in development at all levels— personal, family, communal, national and even global because women are forces to be reckoned with in the society as they are naturally endowed and disposed to educate and nurture children but also to render humane and leadership services in love and unity. The empowerment of women proves significant positive results in various spheres, which include improvement in hygiene and basic health, reduction of infant-child mortality rate, reduction of poverty rate, etc. Education and empowerment of women are therefore a *conditio sine qua non* in accelerating development and ensuring peace. The perception that each person deserves respect, care and love and adhering to it in concrete daily activities in an uninterrupted spin that begins from each single individual and spreads throughout the globe proves a logical and pragmatic tool for lasting global peace.

In the following chapter, we shall delve into a deeper understanding of Edehism as a sustainable African philosophy of life for man and woman everywhere.

CHAPTER FIVE

AFRICAN PHILOSOPHY OF LIFE FOR MAN AND WOMAN EVERYWHERE

By Dr. Charles C. Umeh, Ph.D.

Abstract

Edehism is an African philosophy of life and is being propounded by the Rev. Fr. Prof. E.M.P. Edeh, and put into practical use and application through his numerous projects and establishments scattered all over Nigeria and the entire human race. In this presentation, a panoramic view of the beginning, the progression and the explosive dimensions of Edehism is taken. Then follows "I Have a Dream" for Edehism in Nigeria, Africa and the entire human race in the foreseeable future and thereafter.

Introduction

Let us begin this presentation with a dictionary definition of two relevant words: philosophy and metaphysics. The Longman Dictionary of Contemporary English defines philosophy as (1) the study of the nature and meaning of existence, reality, knowledge, goodness, etc. (2) any of various systems of thought having this as its base, e.g. the philosophy of Aristotle (3) a rule or set of rules for living one's life especially based on one's beliefs and experiences (Longman Dictionary, 1978, p.184). The same dictionary defines metaphysics as (1) a branch of the study of thought (philosophy) concerned with the science of being and knowing (2) any type of thinking at a higher level, which is hard to understand (Longman Dictionary, 1978, p.681).The meanings of these two words go through all that has to be said in this presentation. Edeh is the father of African philosophy and metaphysics. An attempt to take a panoramic view of Edehism at this point in time becomes necessary. Fr. Edeh has been fittingly described as a child of destiny. He was born on 20 May 1947 to the family of Papa Joseph and Mama Elizabeth Omeogo Edeh Ani Onovo at Akpugo in Nkanu-West L.G.A., Enugu State, Nigeria.

Divinely Inspired Beginning:

It was in 1985, during the prolonged aftermath of the Nigerian Civil War that news went round that God has sent a messiah in the person of a young Holy Ghost Priest, Rev. Fr. Edeh who has set up a place in Elele, River's State, where millions of people are receiving peace, reconciliation and rehabilitation.

> Thus in answer to the call of caring he adopted the mission of practical and effective charity with emphases on the sick, the needy, suffering, lonely, abandoned, handicapped and the helpless youths in our society. (Onyewuenyi, R., 2010).

The First Centre for Peace, Justice and Reconciliation in the Christian world was started by Fr. Edeh in Elele, River's State in 1984.The news of this centre and its success in bringing peace and reconciliation to millions of feuding people spread like wild fire.

> The news of Fr. Edeh's meticulous care and resuscitating of the helpless regardless of creed, colour, nationality, ethnic groupings etc. spread from Elele to all over the country and beyond. People began to stream to Elele not only to find food, special care, but shattered and broken families were coming to have their cases peacefully settled and have the warring factions fully reconciled and have peace reign in their hearts (Onyewuenyi, R., 2010, p. 26).

The Reconciliation Ministry in Fr. Edeh's Pilgrimage Centre quickly expanded into six committees and from 1984 to 1996, the recorded number of cases satisfactorily resolved by each of the six committees stand as follows:

i.	Spiritual Director's Office with Fr. Edeh personally presiding	-	1.6 million
ii.	Special Cases Committee	-	972,438
iii.	Lands disputes and Allied Matters Committee	-	1.2 million
iv.	Marriage and Family Squabbles Committee	-	1.4 million
v.	Business disputes and related Conflicts Committee	-	974,114
vi.	General Cases Committee	-	974,230
	Total		6,880,782

The record shows that from 1984 to date 2014 the number of settled cases number more than 14 million.

> It is worthy of note here that a big number of these cases or disputes referred to Fr. Edeh's ministry had been fruitlessly tried several times over, either in the customary courts, before village elders or in State high courts. Through this ministry, Fr. Edeh has presented himself as an enormous agent of peace and reconciliation to millions (Edeh, 2007, pp. 68- 69).

The Progression of Edehism from Its Divinely Inspired Beginning:

As the father of African philosophy and metaphysics, Fr. Edeh set out to practicalise his vision in numerous dimensions of human existence.

> The distinctive feature of African Philosophy is that it cannot be thought of in terms of an objective, abstract science as was fashionable in other world Philosophies. In African philosophy, we are dealing with a practical theoretical science in the sense that by nature African metaphysics is a lived philosophy rather than a purely theoretical or scientific enterprise.

In 1985, Fr. Edeh presented his more than ten-year-old research in his monumental publication titled *Towards an Igbo Metaphysics*. The application of Edeh's philosophy of theory and action (Edehism) propelled him to embark on the establishment of numerous institutions and projects some of which are outlined below:

1. Establishment of private nursery and primary schools where genuine teaching and learning take place for the proper foundation of the child for successful life on earth. The child is given a rounded education that takes care of his or her intellectual and moral wellbeing.

2. Establishment of private secondary schools where secondary education is properly given to the child both male and female. Well-trained and selected teachers are employed to manage the teenage storm and stress that occurs during this period of life. Edeism is inculcated in the child for thinking and doing appropriate things for the good of the child and the larger society.

3. Establishment of private polytechnic where technical and allied education are given to candidates who are technically inclined. In this polytechnic, OSISATECH Polytechnic, students are trained to international standards. There can be no strike by staff or students. There is no selling of handouts. Secret cult is prohibited. There can be no marketing of examination scores. What you get is what you have after marking your script. Students who normally graduate on record time are employed all over the world and they are doing wonderfully well. Thanks to the philosophy of Edehism.

4. Establishment of private college of education- OSISATECH College of Education, where teachers who are inclined to the education industry are properly trained. The modus operandi in Edeh's College of Education is exactly the same with what is obtained in his polytechnic. The watchword is excellence in academics, character and morals.

5. Establishment of two private universities Madonna University with three Campuses at Okija, Elele, and Akpugo (with Elele now as the main campus), and Caritas University at Amorji Nike, Enugu. These two universities are centres of excellence and morals. All the students are made to live only in their university campuses, i.e. off-campus residence is not allowed. There can be no strike or go slow by all staff and students. Secret cult is not allowed. All forms of examination malpractices are not tolerated. Selling of handouts by staff is not allowed. As the result of these disciplinary measures, the students are trouble free and graduate at a record time. Moral decadence and indolence prevalent in other surrounding tertiary institutions are absent in these universities.

6. Establishment of the religious congregation of the fathers of Jesus the Saviour for the training of those who feel called to serve the Lord as Saviourite Priests. Many of them have already been ordained and they are doing very well in the service of Jesus the Saviour and in promoting Edehism, the philosophy of their founder.

7. Establishment of the religious congregation of sisters of Jesus the Saviour for the training of reverend sisters who serve the Lord through total service to the church in whatever direction they are called to served. Large numbers of these sisters of Jesus the Saviour have since been professed and they are rendering wonderful service in continuation of the practical and effective charity to millions who flock from all over the world to the pilgrimage centre for peace in their hearts and families. The Sisters are now spread in Nigeria, Italy, America, London, Germany, Carribbean Island and so on.

8. Establishment of the religious congregation of the male contemplatives of Jesus the Saviour.

9. Establishment of the religious congregation of the female contemplatives of Jesus the Saviour.

    The contemplatives are cloistered, monastic people who deeply pray, meditate and fast to bring down God's mercy on this sinful world.

10. Establishment of health institutions.

    Between 1986 and 2012, Edeh established six categories of health and social welfare institutions. These include:

    i.   1 Maternity hospital at Elele
    ii. 1 Motherless babies home
    iii. 1 rehabilitation centre
    iv. 1 Specialist diagnostic laboratory
    v.   1 medical clinic and
    vi. 1 Teaching hospital

    Plus the Pilgrimage Centre of Eucharistic Adoration (also known as the Pilgrimage Centre of Peace and Reconciliation) (Edeh, 2007, pp. 65).

11. Establishment in Madonna and Caritas Universities F.M. radio stations that broadcast, entertain, and educate the listening public. These F.M. radio stations assist in the training of Mass Communication undergraduates who specialize in broadcasting and the media.

12. Establishment of printing and publishing press Madonna University Press (MUP) that has made a great mark in efficient printing and publishing of scholarly books, articles and other materials.
13. Establishment of Pilgrim Pure Water Company that bottles and packages pure water that most of the time are distributed free of charge during official gatherings such as, during the international conferences, charity food distributions during Easter and New year and other prominent occasions.
14. Establishment of a bakery where bread, biscuits, and other bakery products are hygienically produced and consumed by all and sundry.
15. Establishment of other centres for producing Pilgrim sacramentals such as Pilgrim Balm, Pilgrim Holy Oil, Pilgrim Wine, Pilgrim Car Stickers, etc. Using these sacramentals faithfully while saying the CPM Prayers have resulted in miraculous healings. Many researchers on the Pilgrimage Centre Elele can testify to this claim!

Edeism has continued to make a wonderful, sustainable mark through the establishment of these numerous educational and developmental institutions.

The Explosive Dimensions of Edehism

Edeh's African Philosophy of Thought and Action has already taken an international dimension. The work that codified this African philosophy, *Towards an Igbo Metaphysics,* (1985), E.M.P. Edeh, Loyola University Press Chicago, has already been translated and published in many world languages. Researchers, all over the world have discovered in it a new pattern of thought for sustainable peace and progress in the world. It is a pattern of thought that could bring to an end these reckless shedding of human blood all over the nations of the modern world.

> Cambridge Biological Centre, England, singles Very Rev. Fr. Prof. Emmanuel Edeh as a leading star, and dedicates the first edition of *Outstanding People of the 21st Century* to him for his invaluable contribution to the "Church, Education, and Suffering" (Onyewuenyi, 2010, pp. 132).

In her book *Peace to the Modern Society* (2004), Mother John Bosco Kalu SJS, the Mother General of the Sisters of Jesus the Saviour remarked emphatically that Fr. Edeh is a great contributor to the peace of mankind.

His works and their effects have spread beyond Nigeria and are well established in London (North London, South London, East London, Lewisham, Central London), Germany (Frankfurt, Stutggart, Achen, Cologne, etc.), Holland (Da Hague, Amsterdam, etc.), Austria (Vienna, Gratz, etc.) USA (Detroit, New York, Miami, Chicago, Atlanta, California, etc.), and the Caribbean Islandof St Lucia.

Rev. Fr. Prof. Emmanuel M.P. Edeh C.S.Sp., OFR has collected over twenty national and international honours and awards, which form the Vol.1, Chapter Ten, "Awards and Recognitions of the books, (Onyewuenyi, 2010, pp. 132- 145).

Edehism, African Philosophy of Life and Being - "I Have a Dream"

Comparing the life and works of Edeh, with the life and works of some internationally acclaimed people of the world like Plato, Aristotle, Socrates, Frank Buchman (Moral Re-armament Leader), Maria Theresa of Calcutta, Nostradamus (the man who saw tomorrow), Mahatma Gandhi, Martin Luther King Jr., Nelson Mandela, Desmond Tutuh, Wole Soyinka, etc., one will observe that while each of them has concentrated in only one or two areas of life and existence, Edeh has concentrated on the holistic development of man and woman from infancy to good old age.

Fr. Edeh once bared his heart while addressing the entire staff of Caritas University, that as an ordained priest of the Holy Ghost Congregation all his struggles in life is totally devoted to the betterment of the entire human race; that he has no wife or children to care for but his entire life is devoted to the proper development of the children of the world. He told us that everything he has achieved is for the greater glory of God and the betterment of humanity and that he is doing his best to make the world a better place than he met it when he arrived on May, 20th, 1947, the day the Austrian physicist, Philipp Leonard who won the1905 Nobel Prize in Physics for his research on cathode rays and the discovery of their properties bowed his exit from the world.

I have a dream for Edehism in Nigeria, Africa and the entire human race; a dream of an African Philosophy of Thought and Action which has come to transform Africa and the entire human race. I have a dream of another star shining from Africa to better the entire human race. Whenever I watch him say the Holy Mass, I see the star of miracles descending to cleanse the world. I see healings take place, depression and despair disappearing and a brand new rehabilitated people emerging. I have a dream of a star who has come to render selfless service. The first private university in Nigeria is founded in the name of the fathers of Jesus the Saviour and the second one that followed, is in name of the sisters of Jesus the Saviour. I have a dream of one selfless missionary who has employed millions upon millions of people in his numerous establishments scattered all over Nigeria and the entire human race for no personal gains but all in the service of God and *mmadi*. I have a dream of Edehism, his Philosophy of Thought and Action spreading to all nooks and crannies of the world, making the will of God to be done on earth as it is done in Heaven.

Despite all the storms and stress of life, I have a dream of an African "special humble man of God" (saint), emerging at the end of time and gathering numerous other spectacular Africans of the same around him to heavenly paradise because they all worked selflessly for God's people.

CHAPTER SIX

THE CHARISM OF
FR. EMMANUEL EDEH, C.S.Sp.,
A MAN OF MANY PARTS,
THE GIFT FOR WORLD PEACE

By Fr. Prof. Augustine Onyeneke, C.S.Sp.

Abstract

Fr. Edeh, a charismatic gift to the society has in the religious, educational and secular fields created projects and activities for reconciliation of people and families ravaged by conflicts, healing broken lives and bringing peace and harmony to families and communities.

Fr. Emmanuel Edeh has proved to be multifaceted, a man of many parts making a name in academics to the rank of a professor, having previously obtained a doctorate degree in philosophy from a good American University (De Paul University) in Chicago and making a name in the Igbo Metaphysics.

If the expression "charismatic" is accepted as embodying a flow of exceptional personal competence or ability in an individual, Fr. Emmanuel Edeh has without doubt proved to be a charismatic in Nigeria. His projects on the religious, educational, and secular fields have emerged and are being sustained by an exceptional personal creative ability, which he has, as well as a leadership quality to engage a sustained and committed allegiance of numerous followers in various walks of life who have confidence in his personal exceptional endowment. He is one man able to mobilize teams of loyal and faithful adherents and able to stretch out hands of cooperative engagements across religious and professional boundaries.

Examples:

a. On the religious place he is a practicing Catholic priest of the Holy
    Ghost Congregation, a Spiritan, ordained in 1976, and who made a
    phenomenal leap forward from the 1980s into founding a popular
    movement, the Catholic Prayer Ministry of the Holy Spirit (CPM)
    with headquarters at Elele. He has successfully organized in the
    headquarters a stable network of monthly popular pilgrimages to
    Elele and gained recognition for the Centre as a national pilgrimage
    centre approved by Catholic Bishops Conference of Nigeria (CBCN).
    Alongside the prayer ministry, he has founded multiple male and
    female religious congregations under the spirituality of Jesus the
    Saviour: sisters of Jesus the Saviour, fathers of Jesus the Saviour, male
    contemplatives or monks, and female contemplatives or nuns of Jesus
    the Saviour, and these foundations are scattered out in the Rivers,
    Anambra, and Enugu states.

b. An essential part of the humanitarian ministry and social services of
    Fr. Edeh at Elele are the projects and activities for reconciliation among
    people affected by interpersonal, family and community conflicts,
    healing broken personal lives, and bringing peace and harmony to
    families and communities.

c. He was able to harness the support of a committee of friends for moral
    and material support to undertake projects in the field of Education, and
    thus returning to the footsteps of the previous Spiritan evangelization
    activities in south east Nigeria. With the double support from the
    committee of loyal friends and his new religious congregations, he
    has rapidly established in southeast Nigeria a beehive of primary
    and secondary schools. He has proceeded further and higher than
    in the previous Spiritan history of education in the area into third
    levels of education, into successfully founding a polytechnic and a
    college of education, and in addition, founding two universities, the
    Madonna and the Caritas Universities. Thousands of students have the
    opportunity to go through the schools and be affected and molded by
    the moral and intellectual standards promoted in them and afterwards
    to have the requisite skills for a decent and gainful employment in life.

d. He has also established middle scale, facilities and enterprises for
    producing such items as table water, mineral drinks toiletries, and
    cosmetics, etc. All these, along with the educational institutions, create

employments for many people running into thousands, in different ranges of professional and industrial skills while also supplying vital material needs of society. [For example, the educational project of Madonna University, Akpugo campus alone employs over 300 academic and non-academic staff, with an additional batch of over100 artisans and labourers in construction and cleaning works.]

In the field of education, Fr. Edeh is bound to be remembered for his insistence on the pursuit of quality in education and in morals and the determination to eliminate the errors that crept into the organization of education during the eclipsing military regimes in the country. The conduct of examinations is jealously guarded in ways that are determined to leave no room for the vices of false performance ('expo', impersonation, forgery of results and certificates) and to ensure that examination certificates and the grades of graduates of his schools are true, valid and as much as possible reliable and thus creating and promoting confidence for graduates of his institutions. In the area of morality, every effort is employed to enforce total residence in his institutions for students and a stringent security control to eliminate cult activities and unwholesome social associations among the students. He has the credit for having led the way in the social/political pressures required to make the break-through into government policy in Nigeria to permit private/voluntary agencies (missions and individuals) to establish private universities in Nigeria. For the Spiritans of southeast Nigeria, one can now talk of the Edeh style, which is beyond the established laudable records of his Spiritan Family, the Holy Ghost Fathers of Nigeria, in the pre-independence years.

Conclusion

It is said in holy writ, "Do not consider anyone as blessed before his death, for only then he will be known" (Sirach, pp. 11,28). For his visible laudable accomplishments in Nigeria, Fr. Emmanuel Edeh has been decorated with several social awards: a Nigerian national award of honour of OFR (Order of the Federal Republic) and a special medal of honour from the Vatican, besides decorations by professional groups.

According to a sociological principle established by Max Weber, organizations built on charismatic authority must be 'routinized' to ensure their lasting future beyond the life of the charismatic initiator (Maralambos, 1984, pp. 281). In modern industrial and rational society, a transition is necessary in organization from charismatic (person-oriented) patterns of authority to bureaucratic (rational and office-regulated) processes for charismatic based social movements or organizations to ensure a lasting future beyond the life span of a charismatic founder. These bold project initiatives of Fr. Edeh in the field of education that were initially afloat much at a charismatic and personal manner are currently being sufficiently imbued with relevant and adequate bureaucratic structures and frameworks to ensure their effective survival and progress in the unknown future. All these bold project initiatives are being maintained for the specific purpose of engendering peace in the lives of millions of human beings both male and female regardless of age, colour, and belief, etc.

CHAPTER SEVEN

EDEH'S PHILOSOPHY OF THOUGHT AND ACTION (EPTAISM) AS FOUNDATION FOR CROSS-CULTURAL RELATIONSHIPS AND WORLD PEACE

By Dr. Mike Ike Okwudili, Ph.D

Abstract

Edeh's philosophy of thought and action contemplates socio-cultural issues and matches them with actions that create peace with socio-cultural relationship. This relationship through special and effective charity brings in honesty, justice and respect for the dignity of human person, thus bringing peace to the world at large.

Introduction

The modern day's society is becoming very complex, yet the gap that may exist within and between cultures is narrowing down. Diversities are shrinking and inter-cultural relationships are giving way to cross-cultural relationships. Intermarriages, migrations, enculturation etc are closing national and cultural boundaries. This has resulted in cross-cultural relationships. But the culture of the individual is known to affect his thought process and pattern. This is because; human cultures are created and learned.

To really come to terms with African culture and cultural milieu is to come to terms with African philosophy of life. And to come to terms with African philosophy is to understand African views about reality, about life and existence and about beings and being. This in the words of Edeh (2006) will have to do with the interplay of thought and action pattern. These were reflected in Edeh's (1985) earlier work where he identified and systematically presented African philosophy and African philosophical thought system and pattern. Here he metaphysically presented African culture, language, socio-religious milieu and indeed a holistic view of the way the African views the universe. His notion of *mmadi* or *the good that is* presents man as good within the context of creation, a confirmation of the mystery of man's relation with God. As the father of African philosophy, he posited that African philosophy must be treated holistically to include how the African acts in response to his belief system and thought pattern. Therefore, if man is accepted as good, then realities that establish man as such must be constructed. These realities must be metaphysically focused towards uplifting man from his low state that tends to make man sub-man. This notion extends the beliefs of Mondin (1985), Goleman (1995) and Frick (2003) that man has always produced cultures and realities. This is essentially because he is essentially a cultural and not necessarily a natural animal.

Culture according to Mondin (1985) is a widely used term which historically and currently has three meanings and three principal uses. These are elitarian, pedagogical, and anthropological:

- In the elitarian sense, culture signifies a great quantity of knowledge and experience, either in general or in some particular sector. Thus, for example, one can be said to have philosophical culture, artistic culture etc.
- In the pedagogical sense, culture indicates the education, formation and acculturation of man.
- While in the anthropological sense, culture signifies the totality of customs, techniques, values, belief and belief system, thought and thought pattern that tend to distinguish a social group, a tribe, a people, a nation. This is a model for living in proper society.

Here let me take a critical look at Edeh's Philosophy of Thought and Action (EPTAISM) as a foundation for cross-cultural relationships and world peace.

EPTAISM, Cross Cultural Relationships and World Peace

Man is a cultural being. This entails that at the moment of birth, nature gives an individual hardly the necessary minimum, the essentials to be a human being and assign to him the task of making himself and forming himself so as to fully realize his being through culture. But ultimately, man is good; his formation reflects his socio-cultural environment. Therefore, for him to fully realize his being, his socio-cultural environment must be constructed and ordered. The process of doing this requires constructive thought process, pattern and requisite action to put such into practical realities: Edeh (1985) in *Towards an Igbo Metaphysics* was able to etymologically develop the concept of man as good originating from the creator, the source of being and all goodness (*mmadi*). Therefore, the goodness of human as manifested physically and ontologically is a participation in the goodness of God, who himself is the supreme good.

The notion of man as *mmadi* as elucidated by Edeh's African philosophy is not intended to end as a philosophical speculation, but as a practical demonstration of goodness of man as a foundation for cross-cultural relationships and world peace.

Edeh's Philosophy of Thought and Action (**EPTAISM**) encourages thought process and pattern that contemplates socio-cultural issues and problems such as crisis in the world, and socio-cultural segregation, but does not encourage such contemplations that cannot be matched with actions to end such and create world peace and socio-cultural relationships.

Man is a universal being; the notion of *mmadi* presents him as universally good from God the supreme Good. This notion of universal goodness entails universality of existence and universality of purpose. In the same vain, despite cultural diversities, certain human cultures are universal. These universal cultures represent the features and characteristics of man and manifest things that make all members of the human race alike. EPTAISM and the notion of *mmadi*, or the good that is, present a universal front for appraising humans and for dealing with universal human problems. The essence is to present man as a universal purpose. This will lay a strong foundation for enduring cross-cultural relationships and universal peace, which is anchored on mutual understanding, respect and tolerance.

Man is the centre of all cultures, and therefore a cultural being. According to Taylor (1972), man is a cultural being in two senses. First of all, in the sense that he is the artifice of culture but also, as can always be seen, in that it is himself who is the prime receiver and the greatest effect of culture. Culture in this sense has two principal acceptable meanings here:

- A formation of an individual (subjective sense) and
- A society's spiritual form (objective sense)

This has the goal of the realization of the individual in all his dimensions and in all his capacities. The primary aim of culture then is to cultivate man as a unique example of human species which according to Edeh (2006) represent goodness from God the supreme good. Such unique achievement will help develop universal values, norms and ethics that will prosper cross-cultural relationships and help attain world peace. The objective of culture in accordance with the conclusion of Edeh has always been that of making man a person, a fully developed Spiritual being to complete and perfect the realization of the "man" project which providence assigned to him.

Therefore, man as a cultural being according to Marrou (1966) is not prefabricated; he must take action to construct himself with his own hand and with his innate potentials in positive ways. The ideal thing in the eyes of Plato, Socrates, and the stoics, is to make man a project in himself capable of redefining, redesigning and reconstructing himself and his environment. This idea is congruous with the essence of EPTAISM and both seem to have collectively pursued a process, pattern and action that further the course of man as essentially being with endless faculties to further his own course to bring about peaceful co-existence and world peace. Thus, philosophical anthropologists seem to have collectively adopted as core to their activities, "The Man Project".

It may be on this premise that Pope John Paul II once wrote to the UNESCO representative that culture is that by which man as man becomes more a man and is more drawn closer to being. It is that which bounds the very important distinction between being and having. But culture beyond being an essential property of man is also a factor which distinguishes various national groups, clarifying and specifying them. For instance, culture is what distinguishes an Igbo man of South East from a

Yoruba man of Southwest Nigeria. It also distinguishes the thought process and pattern of the Igbos from those of the Yoruba in quite significant ways. The style and content of the philosophy of various ethnic nationalities are therefore often significantly influenced by their cultural background and the experiences they acquire from being members of that ethnic nationality.

Understanding the property of society in which an individual exists will require x-raying the totality of individuals that characterize a social group. Culture is therefore the life of a group in contacts, institutions, technological equipment, art and music. It will ordinarily show in characteristic concepts and behaviour, customs and traditions, as well as philosophy. Summarily then, it signifies all those things, institutions, material objects and typical reaction to situations that characterize a people and distinguish them from other groups.

These cultural specifics are not static, but are dynamic and flexible. Cross-cultural assimilation of values, norms, ethics and all properties cultural are changing ethnic cultures. This position indicates that cultural changes occur. Such changes among ethnic nationalities are directing cultural development towards universal cultures. This constancy of changes and consistency of development have over the years brought about universalities of culture. This with the proposition of Edeh (2006) and based on his philosophy of universal goodness of man present a strong foundation for the development of cross-cultural relationships and attainment of world peace.

Most anthropologists have recognized the three fundamental components of modern culture as economics, politics and education. The understanding is that with these activities, modern societies confront their needs; with economics, they produce goods and services necessary for its sustenance; with politics, they regulate the rapport between the members of social groups; and with education, it trains and forms their members according to the ideals that have been conserved by the tradition. These are social construct for humanity. **EPTAISM** encourages socio-economic constructs that further the course of man as good. It showcases a philosophy of ideals of human existence and pursues the ideas of human dignity, based on the belief that all being created by God are ontologically good and as such deserve peace, respect, care, love, cross-cultural understanding, and interactions.

Conclusion

Edeh through his Philosophy of Thought and Action has pursued the wellbeing of humans with keen interest. His conception of man as good and the desire to concretize his thought process and pattern into existential reality has led him to construct realities that further the course of man as good. Examples of such realities are:

a. Centre for Peace and Reconciliation
b. Motherless Babies' Home
c. Hospital and Rehabilitation Centres
d. Polytechnic
e. College of Education
f. Universities

The Centre for Peace, Justice and Reconciliation is charged with the task of bringing peace and reconciliation to the heart of the people. The centre has been vital in the development of peace in Nigeria, Africa and the world at large. The dictum is bringing peace to the world through bringing peace to the individual, the sick, the suffering, the abjectly poor, the miserable youth. To Edeh, peace is not just the absence of war, but rather the peace that lasts in the presence of the factors and forces that eliminate and even prevent conflicts and minimize tension. This peace he tries to bring into the world through special and effective charity, which provides justice, honesty, education, morality, health, development and respect for the dignity of the human person irrespective of race, colour, creed, social status and physical conditions. This ultimately will help usher in harmonious existence and cross-cultural relationship, thus bringing peace to the world at large. This brings us to the theme of the next chapter.

CHAPTER EIGHT

EDEH'S UNIVERSITY EDUCATION AND SOCIAL STABILITY

By Prof. Alumode Bernard Ede, Ph.D

Abstract

Education is the backbone of empowerment. Thus Fr. Edeh uses University education as an epitome of social stability as he inculcates in the youths passing through his University institutions the mission of always aspiring for peace wherever they find themselves.````

Introduction

Education is a generic term, which embraces formal, informal and non-formal education. Education can be described as a process, a product, a discipline and an experience. It is the process of teaching, training and learning especially in institutions of learning, to improve knowledge, develop skills and inculcate attitude. It is a product that is seen in a processed individual through teaching, training and learning, thus we can say that Mr. X is a product of Caritas University. Education can also be described as a discipline or subject of study which deals with how to teach: thus, Mr. Y's discipline could be Educational Management. Finally, education can be described as an experience which teaches someone something; hence the dictum "experience is the best teacher."

In this discourse, we are concerned with education as a process: the process of preparing the child to become a contributing member of his society. Thus Fafunwa (1974), defined education as the aggregate of all the processes by which a child or young adult develops his abilities, attitudes and other forms of behaviours which are of positive value to the society in which he lives. This implies that education like socialization is the process of transmitting culture in terms of continuity and growth for disseminating knowledge either to ensure social control or to guarantee rational direction of the society or both.

In its broadest sense, education is simply an aspect of socialization:

It involves the acquisition of knowledge and attitudes and the learning of skills. Whether intentionally or unintentionally, education helps to shape beliefs and moral values. In non-literate societies, education is hard to distinguish from other aspects of life. Young people learn their lessons largely by joining in the social group.

Knowledge and skills are usually learned informally by imitating examples provided by adults. Although adults sometimes instruct their young ones, they do so as part of their daily routine. Thus, boys accompany their fathers to farms while girls assist their mothers with cooking and gathering vegetables. It then follows that whether it is literate or non-literate society, education must go on.

The difference, however, between literate and non-literate societies is that in literate society, the school provides context where skills can be learned. Thus Haralambos and Holborn (2008, p. 600), pointed out that the school is society in miniature, a model of the social system where the child interacts with other members of the society in terms of fixed set of rules. This experience prepares the child for interacting with members of the society as a whole in terms of society rules.

Social stability on the other hand entails state of tranquillity where people live together in peace and unity with little or no rancor (Haralambos & Holborn, 2008, p. 600).Durkhein maintained that society can survive only if there exists among its members a sufficient degree of homogeneity; education perpetuates and reinforces this homogeneity by fixing in the child from the beginning the essential similarities which collective life demands. Without these essential similarities, cooperation, solidarity and therefore social life itself, would be impossible. Individuals therefore, have to learn to cooperate with those who are neither their kin nor their friends. Education provides the link between the individual and society. A vital task for all societies is the welding of a mass of individuals into a united whole, in other words the creation of social solidarity. This involves a commitment to society, a sense of belonging, and a feeling that the social unit is more important than the individual. To become attached to the society, the child must feel in it something that is real, alive, and powerful, which dominates the person and to which he also owes the best part of himself. This is provided through socialization or education. Education, particularly the teaching of history, provides this link between the individual and society. If the history of their society is brought alive to children, they will come to see that they are part of something larger than themselves. They will then develop a sense of commitment to the social group. This then is a major relation between education and social stability.

Role of University Education

Webster admonished that the most dangerous men are educated men without character. Knowledge is not all that education embraces: the feelings are to be disciplined, passions must be restrained, true and worthy motives are to be inspired, profound feelings are to be instilled and pure morality, above all, must be inculcated under every circumstance in order to achieve social stability. Ezeaka pointed out that education is not only the bedrock of any progressive nation but also the backbone of individual empowerment (Ezeaka, 2013, p. 19). No nation thrives economically, politically and otherwise without qualitative and balanced system of education generally and university education in particular.

University education, which is the type of education given after secondary education, has strategic roles to play. Osokoya stated that the aims of University education include developing and inculcating proper values for the survival of the individuals and to become positive contributing members of the society (2012, pp. 115-125). Others are developing the intellectual capability of individuals to understand and appreciate their local and external environments and developing physical and intellectual skills of individuals. Furthermore, they include promoting and encouraging scholarship and community service, promoting national and international unity, understanding and interaction, promoting national development through relevant level manpower training, and solidifying national cohesion and stability.

The end of every level of education is the gradual but continuous perfection of the human being. All human beings are moral, spiritual, intellectual, social, political and economic agents. University education in its true sense must embrace the integral formation and comprehensive development of the human person. Today, unfortunately, university education and morality have been divorced one from the other. However, if the intellect is trained at the negligence of the will, the result, at best, is the production of intelligent tyrants, which leads to social disintegration (instability). If, on the other hand, the will is trained at the expense of the intellect, the result is ignorant men of goodwill. It follows, therefore, that for any university to worth the name cannot but provide for those they are hatching: a balanced programme of training which avoids tyrants and ignorant men of good will. It is this divorce of university education from morality that prompted Fr. Edeh to establish his universities. As Unegbu put it, through these educational institutions, Fr. Edeh has most effectively set out to correct the evils that have long since destroyed and ridiculed the entire Nigerian educational system (Edeh, 2007, p. 78). This then is the focus of this discourse: Edeh's University Education and Social stability.

Fr. Edeh and the Establishment of Tertiary Institutions

The Nigerian civil war broke out in 1967 and lasted for three years. As a result of the civil war, the Nigerian educational system was crippled especially in the Eastern states which were the war zone. The after effect of the war did not augur well for the future of the Nigerian milieu. This led Otite (1995) to say that gun-based and gun-controlled styles of social relationships became part of Nigerian society. Alimba and Awodoyin (2008) remarked that Nigeria's university environments became highly volatile because of the easy flow of arms into the system and the abnormal ways they have been used to perpetuate different kinds of crime, namely secret cultism, strikes, and riots among students and staff, and other types of social ills. The existence of intimidation in universities in Nigeria made Agekameh (2001) to call them 'threats of war'. He said that the orgy of violence often witnessed in university campuses was due to the ways students freely brandished pistols or revolvers and used them to unleash terror on fellow students and staff.

Based on these societal ills and other salient reasons, Edeh went into the establishment of institutions of higher learning.

- 1989   Our Saviour College of Education; and
- 1989   Our Saviour Institute of Science, Agriculture and Technology (OSISATECH) Polytechnic. These were the first non-government owned (private) College of Education and Polytechnic in Nigeria.
- 1993   Madonna University was established with Anambra State law
- 1999   Madonna University, the first private University in Nigeria and the first Catholic University in West Africa, came to be with Federal Government Law
- 2004   Caritas University, Amorji-Nike, Enugu.

On the establishment of these institutions, Edeh (2007) had this to say, "It was in the face of the above circumstances (social instability) that I struggled from 1989 till date and established with government approval and certification these institutions." Madonna University has Campuses at three different locations in Okija, Anambra State, and Elele in Rivers State and Akpugo in Enugu State. In his remark, Unegbu said, "Rev. Fr. Edeh has through his universities provided care for the abjectly poor, the troubled youths of the society some who through Fr. Edeh's education support are given the opportunity to avail themselves of proper, sound and functional education" (Edeh, 2007, p. 79). The result of this is proper human development that brings peace to the hearts of the youths as well as less privileged of the society and national stability for all.

In his testimony, John Kanem succinctly stated that as a result of social problems of low standard of education, selling of marks, cultism, immorality, and societal instability, Fr. Edeh set up four educational institutions including two universities to address the problems (Edeh, 2007, p. 79). He went further to say that Madonna University, a university with a difference, is the first of the two universities of Edeh and the first private university to take off in the country. Through the University, Kanem continued, and other educational institutions, Edeh ushered in a reformation for good in the entire educational system in Nigeria: sound, effective and functional education, devoid of secret cultism and strikes, examination malpractice etc. Caritas University was established with the same objectives and focus as Madonna University. Kanem concluded by stating that the education offered in these universities has brought and continues to bring peace and reconciliation to the beneficiaries. They have produced graduates with holistic education: education that encompasses morals, sound academics, humility and transparency.

Merits of Edeh's University Institutions

There is no doubt that Edeh's special university institutions have been creating much impact on the economic, social, political and religious lives of people of different walks of life in Nigeria and beyond. Edeh was aware that without proper and qualitative education, the youths would be left to wallow in crime that peace would not rein supreme, and that society would be left in total disintegration, hence his daring into the establishment of these institutions.

Fr. Edeh's social philosophy as noted by Ezechi is centred on man (Ezechi, 2013, p. 37). The universities, which can be rightly described as special universities, are based on peace education. They are planned for total development of man in body and soul, and they are committed to transmit moral values which go concurrently with qualitative education. The need to reassess universities' commitment to the realization of their goals was one of the forces behind Edeh's establishment of Madonna and Caritas Universities. The violent nature of the youths, armed robbery, killing, arson, prostitution, rape, vandalism and a host of other ills have been the order of the day. To overhaul the situation so that sanity could reign, Edeh found recourse to university education where peace and national stability would reign supreme.

Edeh's university education is fundamental in moderating unwanted behaviour. The aim to change the physical, intellectual, emotional and spiritual abilities of people within the context of their cultural, political and social milieus for sustainable social stability was considered paramount. Peace education conveys the cultivation of peaceful attitudes in its receivers and creates conducive climate in schools and society. In the view of Alimba, peace education is a multifaceted educational programme that encompasses different approaches capable of transforming the behavioural patterns of people (Alimba, 2012, pp. 115-129). This can be achieved through the inculcation of desirable knowledge, attitudes and skills for effective contribution to the cultural, economic and political development, which lead to social stability. Edeh's university programmes are structured accordingly. The programmes are geared towards the promotion of knowledge; skills, attitudes and values needed to bring about behavioural changes that will enable children; youth and adults prevent conflict and bring about social stability.

Edeh's universities have special enabling characteristics that make prototype for social stability. In these universities, emphasis is on character moulding, there is no cultism, no strikes, no students' demonstrations, and no examination malpractices. There is compulsory boarding for all students; rules are enforced and punishment meted on offenders, an act that reflects the seriousness of damage done to the social group by the offence. This helps to make clear to transgressors why they are being punished. In this way, students come to learn that it is wrong to act against the ,interests of the social group as a whole. They learn to exercise self-discipline not only because they would avoid being punished but also because they would come to see that misbehaviour brings about conflict in the society.

Durkhein puts it this way: "It is by respecting the school rules that the child learns to respect rules in general, that he develops the habit of self-control and restraint simply because he should control and restrain himself" (Haralambos & Holborn 2008, p. 600). It is a first initiation into the austerity of duty. Society can thus survive if there exists among its members a sufficient degree of homogeneity. This is achieved through fixing in the child from the beginning essential similarities which collective life demands. Some of the skills, knowledge and attitudes that are propagated by Edeh's universities for transformation of youths and adults are presented in tabular form.

Fig. 1: Basic Skills, Knowledge and Attitudes for Transforming Students Life in Edeh's Universities.

Skill	Knowledge	Attitude
Critical thinking	Knowledge of issues relating to;	Self respect
Problem solving	Self awareness	Honesty
Self solving	Peace and conflict	Open mindedness
Self awareness/reflection	Justice and power	Fair play
Assertiveness	Human rights	Obedience
Reading	Globalization	Caring
Orderliness	Duties and rights of citizens	Empathy
Perseverance	Environment/ecology	Tolerance
Cooperation	Social justice and power	Adaptation
Cheerfulness	Non violence	Sense of solidarity

Figure 1 shows the skills, knowledge and attitudes which students who pass through Edeh's universities acquire. The acquisition of these values empower people to embrace peace, live for peace and work for peace anywhere they find themselves; this leads to social stability. The implication is that university education in Edeh empowers the youths and adults with attitude, skills, and knowledge which, according to him, help them to:

-   Build, maintain and restore relationships at all levels of human interaction
-   Develop positive approaches towards dealing with conflicts from personal to the international level
-   Create a safe environment, both physically and emotionally that nurtures each individual
-   Create a safe world based on justice and human rights, and Build a sustainable environment and protect it from exploitation and war (Harris, 2004, pp. 5-14)

Summary and Conclusion

This research x-rayed the impact of University Education in Edeh on social stability and described education as a generic term that encompasses all aspects of human endeavour. Education is said to be synonymous with socialization as it transmits the culture of the society. It is the backbone of individual empowerment which enables nations to thrive socially, economically, politically and religiously. University education is expected to develop individuals and inculcate right values for survival of the individuals so as to become positive contributing members of society.

Edeh's University education depicts an epitome of instrument for social stability. It is based on peace education, which empowers people with skills, attitudes, and knowledge that are germane for the inculcation of peaceful behaviour and the promotion of a culture of peace and stability in a society. Thus, the general purpose of university education in Edeh is about how to cultivate a culture of peace in people and to promote it in a society. University education in Edeh is structured to build the elements of peace in youth. Peace, of course, is planned and prepared for. In Edeh's university education, peace is planned because peace cannot fall from heaven like manna. Thus, in order to empower youths in Nigeria for peace, university education and other tertiary education as well as other levels of education in Nigeria need to be transformed so that children, youths and adults alike receive the expected skills, knowledge and attitudes required to function effectively in the society.

This is what Edeh has well achieved in his extensive University education programs with immense success resulting in the provision of peace to the millions of youth that have passed and will continue to pass through his Universities and other tertiary institutions.

CHAPTER NINE

EDEH'S PHILOSOPHY IN MORAL EDUCATION AND WORLD PEACE

By Anyahuru Ada

Abstract

This is a critical exposition of Edeh's Philosophy of Action and Doing, which stems from his belief that African philosophy is a lived philosophy, which he expressed through moral education that permeates all his established schools in Nigeria, as a practical approach to world peace. Hence, in a nutshell, this research buttresses the fact that Edeh's philosophy in moral education is indeed a lasting panacea to leading man to his final destination of world peace.

Introduction

Humankind is currently confronted with a paradoxical situation when considering why it has not so far experienced lasting peace in the world. Our specie possesses traits and characteristics that seemingly should provide a basis for world peace, such as generosity, respect for the rights of others, cooperation, and concern for nature and the environment. However, we also possess traits which stand in the way of our realizing peace on any scale, from individual to domestic to national and international. These traits include selfishness, lack of respect for the rights of others, competition, and desire to expand our own sphere of life at the expense of both others and environment (Salk, 1992). Suffice it to say that peace had eluded mankind, considering the present situation of world peace.

Achieving the needed peace therefore calls for attention to that type of education that revolves around the morals and values of individuals.

Moral Education for the Achievement of World Peace

Moral education is the guidance and teaching of good behaviour and value. Morals are important in education because people with solid internal sense of right and wrong are less easily coerced by others. It helps in building good character. It is character education.

World peace is an ideal of freedom, peace and happiness among and within all nations and people. World peace is also used to refer to a cessation of all hostility amongst all humanity (Ayn, 1966, pp. 5-7).

Moral education is the key to uniting nations, bringing human beings closely together. In many parts of the world, civil society suffers because of situations of violent conflicts and war. It is therefore important to recognize the crucial role of education in contributing to building a culture of peace and condemning instances in which education is undermined in order to attack democracy and tolerance.

A culture of peace and non-violence goes to the substance of fundamental human rights which includes social justice, democracy, literacy, respect, dignity for all, international solidarity, respect for workers' rights, equality between men and women, cultural identity and diversity, indigenous peoples and minorities rights etc.

In 2000, the then UNESCO Director General, Federico Mayor, stressed that

> *"Education is not only a vast repository of experience, it also has the know-how and talent to implement innovation and change far beyond what is normally found in government circles. Education…can work to achieve the common goals of an educated, intellectually curious and participatory culture of peace and democracy".*

Education no doubt is a key tool to combating poverty, promoting peace, social, justice, human rights, democracy, cultural diversity and environment awareness. Education for peace which can also be referred to as moral education implies an active concept of peace through values, life skills and knowledge in a spirit of equality, respect, empathy, understanding and mutual appreciation among individuals, groups and nations (Narvaez, 2006, pp. 703-733).

The moral educational action for promoting the concept of world peace concerns the content of education and training, educational resources and material, school and university life. A culture of peace must take root in the classroom from early age. It must continue to be reflected in the curricula at secondary and tertiary levels. However, the skills for peace and non-violence can only be learned and perfected through practice. This involves providing people, with an understanding of and respect for universal values and rights.

Therefore, morals and morality pervade every aspect of our lives (Bull, 1969, pp. 3-5). Every society is concerned about fostering moral character in children and forming responsible citizens (Wynne & Ryan, 1993, pp. 20-30). Moral education is the process of acquiring the values, the knowledge and developing the attitudes, skills and behaviour to live in harmony with oneself, with others, and with the natural environment.

So, values and morals are a set of principles or standards of behaviour. They give meaning and strength to a person's character by occupying a central place in one's life. Moral education reflects one's personal attitudes and judgments, decisions and choices, behaviour and relationships, dreams and vision. Values guide people to do the culturally appropriate things. They are the guiding principles of life and give directions, bring joy, satisfaction and peace. Moral education no doubt brings quality to life as it becomes an internal guidepost. It is needed at all levels of education for a global world peace (Kohlberg, 1984, pp. 5-7).

Edeh's Philosophy of Thought and Action in Moral Education: A Practical Approach to World Peace

Over the course of history, humans have faced numerous obstacles to their survival. Early on, the problems of greatest importance were those concerned with our relationship with the natural environment: Our ability to secure adequate supplies of food, energy and water, to provide clothing and shelter, and to control disease. Overtime, we have accumulated knowledge, and developed technologies which, if adequately applied, appear capable of dealing with these major categories of problems.

Nevertheless, in spite of man's accumulated knowledge, humankind continues to suffer not only from material shortages but also from unhappiness caused by inter-human conflicts, that is, our relationship with our own kind. Indeed, our inability to relate optimally with each other appears to be largely responsible for the continued problems we face with respect to establishing a fully rewarding and harmonious relationship with our environment which has resulted in war and conflict (Groff & Smoker, 1996). No doubt, war and conflicts stem from the persistence of an emphasis on value systems which are optimal to human survival. Therefore, the emergence of an increasing emphasis on values of cooperation and mutualism appears necessary to ensure the establishment and maintenance of peace in the world.

Based on the above viewpoint, practical experiences had shown that Edeh's Philosophy of Thought and Action in moral education has served as a practical approach to achieving world peace.

It is obvious that while African thinkers and philosophers were describing African philosophy, Fr. Edeh went into doing it. Edeh's Philosophy of Thought and Action is a concrete realization of African Philosophy, which is a lived philosophy that must be expressed in practical terms (Edeh, 2007, pp. 1,4,6). As a man that thinks in activity, Fr. Edeh did not stop at theorizing about the participatory goodness of man. In the "good in man," he argues that:

> *"For the Igbos, the notion of "good" is derived from divine creation. To say that man is the "good that is" is not to say that man is "good in se", for no one is "good in se" except God. This is made manifest in such Igbo expression as "So Chukwu di mma na ezie", that is, "Only God is good in the true sense."*

By implication, man is the 'good that is', a being participating in God, the 'good in se'.

He argues that since man is 'good that is', participating in the 'good in se', man is obliged to show maximum care, respect and love to human life. This was what led to Fr. Edeh's vision of practical and lived African philosophy. Edeh's philosophy is born out of his active involvement in presenting to the world African philosophical thought pattern, which is a unity of theory and action. Thus, with African philosophy that stems from African culture, language, socioreligious milieu, and above all, a holistic view of the universe, Fr. Edeh arrived at the ideal understanding of human life and its dignity as it is grounded in the fact that man is ontologically good because he is created by God who is "good in se" and deserves nothing but care and respect (Edeh, 2010).

He therefore insists that the dignity and essence of man must be expressed in practical terms. As such, he posits that "man's dealing with God must permeate truly from God-man relationship to man-man relationship". Thus, Fr. Edeh states:

> *"If God as 'Osebuluwa' cares and supports man to the realization of his purpose I must care for and support my fellow man to the realization of his purpose and this leads to peace in his heart, peace in the society and to the modern world".*

Based on the above, Fr. Edeh, after his intellectual sojourn outside the shores of this country, adopted the mission of practical philosophy. As a man that thinks in activity, he envisioned a world where everyone would live up to the "good in man" (*mmadi*) by establishing an A-Z educational system which is anchored on achieving decency in education and moral excellencies so that more and more people especially the youths can live at peace with their fellow humans and environment wherever they find themselves.

There is therefore no doubt that Edeh's lived Philosophy of Thought and Action in moral education is an epitome of practical approach to the achievement of world peace:

-   In that moral education which can be likened to peace education is integrated in every one of his established institution in the country, ranging from nursery to polytechnic and universities.
-   In that moral education is inculcated in Fr. Edeh's established institutions which also focus on life's skills, covering human rights, international understanding, tolerance, non-violence, multiculturalism and all other values.
-   In that, in all his established institutions in Nigeria, it is noted and observed that everyone including children and students from the

minorities and the disabled learn together with the objective of promoting equal opportunities, thereby achieving peace in their lives.
- In that, since inception of all Fr. Edeh's established schools in the country, there have never been any record of riots, unrests, demonstrations, cultism or strike. As a matter of fact, all his schools are safe and secure to ensure the best possible situation for teaching and learning, thereby facilitating an atmosphere where children and students can learn. Even the teachers and lecturers perform their job in a positive, healthy and safest setting.

Suffice it to say that all Fr. Edeh's schools, ranging from nursery, to primary, secondary, polytechnic and universities can sincerely be referred to as SAFE SANCTUARIES and ZONES OF PEACE.

Through Fr. Edeh's lived Philosophy of Thought and Action, he has consciously imbibed moral education in every level of his established educational and academic system. Surely, his is a lived philosophy!

Above all, Edeh's philosophy of moral education led to his establishment of a centre for peace, justice and reconciliation where millions of cases have been peacefully settled after many efforts in law courts had failed. Through this centre, myriads of families in discord and business partners have been reconciled. As a man whose life is guided by the principle of practical philosophy, Fr. Edeh, as a humble man of God is directly involved in making peace, as he meets with families having such problems, listens to them with love and passion, and offers advice which is moral education in itself (Edeh, 2010).

It is the moral education principles initiated in the schools that are fully implemented in the centre for peace, justice and reconciliation and through this peace is poured into the hearts of millions. Through the deep-rooted moral education in his educational institutions coupled with the activities of peace in the centre for peace, justice and reconciliation Fr. Edeh has succeeded in his effort in engineering and fostering peace in the lives of modern world.

Conclusion

World peace no doubt has eluded mankind, yet every society is concerned about fostering moral character in the younger generations (Wynne & Ryan, 1993).

To this end, if Fr. Edeh's philosophy of action and doing and his concept of the *mmadi* is imbibed, as can be seen in the values and morals that exist in all his established schools in Nigeria, and in his centre for peace, justice and reconciliation, then the peace which has eluded the world for centuries would be realized and man would be led to the promised land of world peace.

CHAPTER TEN

ENGINEERING EDUCATION FOR OUR TIME: FR. EDEH'S SINGULAR CONTRIBUTION TO WORLD PEACE THROUGH TECHNOLOGICAL DEVELOPMENT

By Prof. Onyema E. Uzoamaka, Ph.D.

Abstract

Through Eptaism Edeh has set the Engineering Faculty of the Prestigious Madonna University on a very exciting mission to rescue Nigeria technologically. This will result in the overdue awaited development which will bring peace in the hearts of those involved in engineering and technology.

Introduction

For too long, our people, our nation and our continent have been avid consumers of the fruits of a world technology to which we contribute very little. We have watched the first and second industrial revolutions pass by without active participation. The Information Technology revolution is now here with us. This revolution is still in its infancy. Many problems have been solved, but many more need to be solved to realize its promise. We see a window of opportunity to actively participate in this revolution and leapfrog to join the community of industrialized nations.

Our founding father, the Rev. Fr. Prof. E.M.P. Edeh, was burdened by this prospect, and he decided to do something for our fatherland and posterity.

After consultations with different bodies, the solution he offered is to establish an institution for Engineering Education in the mold of MIT (Massachusetts Institute of Technology)in Cambridge, Massachusetts, USA, recognized as the best engineering school in the world. Fr. Edeh's approach was to excise the Faculty of Engineering from Elele Campus and move it to a remote, pristine and solitary place—an environment for serious thinking, acquire state-of-the-art equipment for the laboratories and workshops—recruit bright and truly talented engineers and set them free to explore the unknown with the watch words THINK, CREATE, MAKE, and INNOVATE.

Our circumstance, if not unique, is at least special. We are at a critical juncture in our history. While we must acknowledge the powerful influence of our heritage, we cannot continue on the path of the past. Indeed, the crucial test of our time lies in the potential of all our institutions to make radical adjustments to embrace and contribute to technological change.

As we adapt to change, as we respond to an expanding array of proposals and opportunities, we should make our choices and decisions within a firm framework, within a clearly defined structure of ideas and values. To participate in the current information technology revolution, our efforts are being channeled through manpower development, rigorous goal oriented research, and useful systems development. By force of circumstance, there must be a PARADIGM SHIFT in our engineering and technological education. Emphasis must now be on THOROUGH UNDERSTANDING OF FUNDAMENTALS, LEARNING BY DOING, RESEARCH, AND DEVELOPMENT.

a. The New Learning Process

Our strategy in training students now, or the learning process, is a shift from acquisition of specialized knowledge to instill in each student the realization that his or her intellectual growth and subsequent success are directly related to the depth of understanding of basic principles. Achieving mastery of basic principles develops the mind as no mere acquisition of specialized knowledge can. It provides the power to attack unsolved problems with success and to explore new areas of knowledge with confidence.

Emphasis on fundamentals and on self-reliance is central in our academic programs to give students a sound command of basic principles, a versatility of mind, insight and perspective concerning natural phenomena, the habit of continued learning, and the power that comes from a thorough and systematic method of attack. From these attributes comes the best assurance against professional obsolescence especially in today's world of rapid technological change, and guaranteed productive professional life. Every subject taught in our faculty is influenced by the environment of a scientific and engineering community: a sense of the quantitative and analytical, a critical analysis of cause and effect, a demand for precision and a powerful curiosity about things not understood.

b. Research

Indeed, research is the primary generator of fresh thoughts, new ideas and intellectual vitality. It is usually the magnitude of research effort that differentiates the present from the past. We are where we are today, partly because of the absence of serious and rigorous research in our institutions. This, we seek to remedy. The equipment in our laboratories and workshops are now put to more use both for training students and for conducting research. To better use the equipment we already have, more staff are being recruited and even more laboratories are being established.

Teaching and research both fulfill our quest to participate in the technological revolution, our desire to understand and effect our environment and advance the frontiers of knowledge. Both activities carried on together have greater power than either performed alone. Research also makes special contribution to our faculty's educational program by providing experience in theory and experiment for both students and staff, and by assuring that classroom teaching is up-to-date.

c. Systems development

We have waited too long to key into the maxim "THINK, CREATE, MAKE, AND INNOVATE". For meaningful social and economic development to take place in Nigeria, we must have the capacity to build systems that enhance our lives. Some of our research findings must be translated into systems that solve our problems and positively impact our lives. Staff and students are encouraged to use the laboratories and workshops not just for experiments, but also to develop systems.

d. Academic Staff

We have taken as our special charge the useful application of science, which is engineering. We are concerned primarily with the rational processes of the mind. We deal in large measure with facts and figures, with elements that are tangible and concrete, development of systems that enhance our lives. These works of science and technology will constitute our own special contribution to the development of Nigeria. Our staff also recognizes that we shall be failing in our duties, if we do not by precept and example inculcate in our students the capacity to cognize and appreciate the finer things in life-the first rate.

But, of course, only through a brilliant and gifted academic staff are we able to impart the highest quality to our manifold undertakings. Thus, the Founder, Fr. Edeh has spared no effort to recruit the brightest and the best. I must say, we are extremely proud of our academic staff. These are men and women who acquired their knowledge in some of the world's best engineering schools and have a proven record of achievement in industry and academics. There is also an intangible attraction whose importance looms very large in the ultimate, critical decision to work here. That intangible attraction embodies the spirit of the institution—the physical and intellectual environment, the opportunities for scholarly work and professional development. The quality of that environment, the climate for scholarship always demands our constant attention and concern.

e. The Student Body

Our student body is exemplary. Free from cultism and many distractions prevalent in other universities. Being a relatively new faculty in the Nigerian University system, our students are free of many of the constraints that come normally with age and tradition. There is an enthusiasm for new projects, a willingness to experiment, a freedom from prejudice that are the mark of youth. These are qualities that have made our faculty an enormously interesting and exciting place to be.

f. Academic Environment

We can never forget that the special role of a university is to offer a haven and intellectual climate in which the highly creative and highly individual scholar can fruitfully pursue his own course in his own way with the esteem of his peers. The climate for action must allow a place for serenity and reflection to stimulate and encourage individual peaks of scholarly achievement. One may not find a better place than the remote, pristine and solitary village Akpugo. The import of these comments carries beyond the realm of the academic staff. They bear directly on our need also, to create an environment that brings out the innate originality of the student that develops his imagination that encourages him to strike out intellectually upon his own. There is no one subject, no special curriculum that fulfills these requirements. They derive only from the style of the institution, from its own spiritual and intellectual ambiance, from all the forces which modulate, temper, and fortify both talent and character. This is the kind of environment that we must never cease to cultivate.

g. Laboratories, Workshops and Studios

The envisaged paradigm shift to "learning by doing" puts emphasis on laboratories, workshops and studios. At present, we have a general engineering workshop, two studios and twenty-three laboratories. Most departments have state-of-the-art equipment in their laboratories. Plans are at advanced stage to establish more laboratories to better support our programs.

h. Library

With holdings in excess of four thousand volumes, five hundred journals and magazines, and e-library with vast subscriptions, our libraries are a vital resource for the support of both teaching and research.

i. Physical Environment

The physical environment also exerts a subtle influence upon the whole community. The on-going effort to improve the quality of architecture, the care and design of our Campus, the evidence of taste and style, are important in giving distinction to our campus, thanks to our founding father Rev. Fr. Prof. E.M.P. Edeh. Indeed, they reflect in large measure its inherent educational philosophy and its concern for the human element in accordance with the mind of the founder.

j. Vision Statement

It is our vision that in the not too distant future, our faculty will be widely known for its contributions to new knowledge, achievements of a remarkable research enterprise which is shared broadly by faculty and students. The interlocking of research and teaching will give us an intellectual climate of extraordinary excitement, a spirit of ferment, and creative innovation which every student may share. We shall be realizing our dream of THINK, CREATE, MAKE, AND INNOVATE and in the process contribute positively to Nigeria's technological endeavours with the attendant economic growth and development. This is the vision of the founder of the prestigious Madonna University.

Concluding Remarks

At present, our faculty is home to the following departments:

- Chemical Engineering
- Civil Engineering
- Electrical/Electronic Engineering
- Food Science Technology
- Mechanical Engineering
- Petroleum Engineering

Arrangements are at advanced stage to introduce the following departments:

- Aeronautical and Astronomical Engineering
- Polymer/Textile Engineering
- Information and Communication Technology.

These programs are supported with well-equipped libraries, laboratories, and workshops. Some of our laboratories, notably the Electronics and Communication Lab, Power and Instrumentation Lab, Computer Lab, Chemical Reaction Lab, Computer Aided Design Lab, Analytical Lab, and

Engineering Workshop have been adjudged among the best in the nation by the regulating agency.

Among Engineering Faculties in Nigerian Universities, the Faculty of Engineering and Technology, Madonna University is *suigeneris*. It is set apart by history, by its own style, by its approach to learning and by its avowed objectives. It was founded on a plan of extra-ordinary clarity, firmness and charity. A plan that contemplated a faculty of well-defined but limited objectives which reflected strongly the philosophical views of the founding father, the Rev. Fr. Prof. E.M.P. Edeh.

What the faculty offers the student is a total experience—an experience that goes beyond the formal curriculum, beyond a programme of courses and series of examinations. It is more than lectures and laboratory work, however excellent they may be. It is the sum of the associations with faculty, all the friendships that are formed among classmates. It is the maturity that comes from participation in student activities, the new perspectives awakened by visiting lecturers and professors. It is the experience of living as part of a community—a community that shares a common concern for things of the mind and the spirit and the sorry state of our technological development.

Our faculty maintains a commitment to foster for its student those qualities of intellect and character which distinguish truly educated men and women, the qualities of responsibility and ethic which mark the professional estate. And of course, we shall be judged not only by the quality of our students' intellectual discipline but by the firmness of their moral fiber, by their attitudes toward the whole of learning, by the manner in which they speak and act, and by their understanding of the obligations of a good citizen.

The Rev. Fr. Prof. E.M.P. Edeh has dispatched us on a very exciting mission to try to rescue Nigeria technologically. We are confident that the outcome of this paradigm shift in engineering education based on Edeh's Philosophy of Thought and Action will ensure mission success.

CHAPTER ELEVEN

THE TOPOLOGY OF PEACE IN THE INFORMATION AGE

By Dr. Atabong T. Agendia-Abanda, Ph.D.

Abstract

The topology of peace is conceived from Edeh's charity peace model, which has been extensively debated at various international conferences. Like a topology in mathematics, computer science, and many other disciplines, which is centred on properties such as connectedness, continuity, and boundedness, the topology of peace as seen in the light of the Edeh's Charity Peace Model (ECPM) is established and managed for the existential realities of connectedness, continuity and completeness. Specific concrete realities of Edeh are researched on a general perspective, with keen interest on the relationships between Edeh's Charity Peace Model (ECPM) the topology of space and communication as in the Education of Mathematics and Computer Science respectively. In the education of computer science and related disciplines, some statistics are presented on the concrete realities of Edeh in the fields of Computer Science, Computer Education and Computer Science/Information Technology. This research also establishes the link between the professional ethics applied by Edeh in the charity peace model in the training of computer and information scientists and those of the institute of computer ethics as drafted in the ten commandments of computer ethics for trained computer professionals. It was found that, over 1800 youths benefitted from the complete training offered by tertiary institutions in varied computer related disciplines for the information age. As a matter of fact, these young adults have established themselves in all works of life, including aviation, production and banking, media, information technology, and communication industries.

KEYWORDS: *EPTAISM, Edeh, network topology, peace, topological spaces, topology*

1. Introduction

Topology is derived from ancient Greek, referring to "place" and "study". It was adopted in mathematics and defined as the mathematical study of shapes and spaces. It is since considered as a major area of mathematics as well as computer science concerned with the most basic properties of space like connectedness, continuity and boundedness (Listing, 1848, p. 67). Topology specifically studies those properties of a system that are preserved under continuous deformations including stretching and bending, but not tearing or gluing. Ideas that are now classified as topological were expressed as early as 1736. Toward the end of the 19th century, a distinct discipline developed, referred to in Latin as the *geometria situs* (geometry of place) or *analysis situs* (Greek-Latin for *picking apart of place*). This later acquired the name topology (Tait, 1883, pp. 316-317).

2. Relationship between the Pilgrimage Centre for Peace, Justice and Reconciliation and Mathematical Topology

The properties of connectedness, continuity and boundedness form a basis for the Pilgrimage Centre for Peace and Reconciliation. This Centre connects people of diversified culture through the father of African philosophy to God. Through the Educational, Health and Charismatic institutions created by Edeh as justified in the book "Peace to the modern world", people feel and get connected to their existential realities. Therefore, in the light of connectedness, the Pilgrimage Centre is a topology. When people become too poor, too sick, too disturbed, too troubled, too bewitched, and too empty, they feel the pressure to take their own life. They generally feel as the world has come to an end. The Pilgrimage Centre for Peace, Justice and Reconciliation offers a sense of continuity to these persons. The rehabilitation unit, reconciliation units and the unit for effective charity is a condition *sine qua non* of the establishment for continuity of any problem-class of people. The connectedness of the Pilgrimage Centre for Peace, Justice, and Reconciliation also justifies the continuity of this ideology. Because of its continuity, the Pilgrimage Centre is a topology. Bounded models have been used to check safety and proved that safety could be obtained faster from accelerated boundedness (Strichman, 2004). As Rocha put it, "The value of the counter example and safety properties generated by Bounded Model Checkers to create test case and to debug systems, is highly recognized" (Rocha, 2010). As a system, the

Pilgrimage Centre for Peace and Reconciliation implements a number of safety properties for its community and as such has achieved boundedness. The unit for justice, the unit for security, the defence units, the Marian Shrine, and Jesus the Saviour in the Eucharist put together have achieved safety for pilgrims, students, lecturers, visitors and the community at large. The Pilgrimage Centre for Peace and Reconciliation is a topology.

The Pilgrimage Centre for Peace and Reconciliation topology has a number of motivating insights like mathematical topology where all shapes and structures are similar in the sense that they may have different physical appearance but the same logical characteristics. Mathematicians will tell you that generally most geometric problems depend not on the exact shape of the object involved, but rather on the way they are put together. In the light of Edeh's Philosophy of Thought and Action, structures do not depend on how it was put, how it looks but what it is used for. For example, the square and the circle have many properties in common: they are both one-dimensional object (from a topological point of view) and both separate the plane into two parts, the part inside and the part outside (Poincare, 1895, pp. 1-123).

2.1: Neighbourhood in the Topology of Peace

One fact of the notion of topological space is to give a convenient and general setting for the notion of continuity of functions. The most intuitive definition and most closely related to notions of topological spaces is in terms of neighbourhoods. Neighbourhood in African philosophy is peace in the special sense that where there is brotherhood (neighbourhood) there is peace. When brotherhood is destroyed, there is conflict. As a popular African musician put it, "Our forefathers were together and when the whiteman came, he divided and separated them, caused confusion, and took their land." Like neighbourhood in topological space, the most elegant and most useful property of such a space is defined in terms of open sets (charity). In the light of EPTAISM, Charity is a well-established and un-separable entity. Combining these two properties of topological space shows that the "Pilgrimage Centre for Peace and Reconciliation" is a topological space. Since models are expected to be defined on appropriate space, the Edeh's Charity Peace Model can be defined on a topological space. This topology, we call the "topology of peace."

The topology of peace in the topological space of the Pilgrimage Centre for Peace and Reconciliation has satisfied some of the equivalent properties of a mathematical topological space as follows:

1. The empty human being, abjectly poor, divided minded, the disabled (multiple organ failure, including a retarded brain). CPM, Pilgrimage Centre and all the members of the Centre are members of the topology of peace.
2. Uniting any sub-collection of the topology of peace is a member of the Pilgrimage Centre for Peace and Reconciliation.
3. The intersection of any sub-collection of the topology of peace is a member of the Pilgrimage Centre for Peace and Reconciliation

2.2 Openness and Closeness in the Pilgrimage Centre for Peace, and Reconciliation Topological Space

The ideology (philosophy of *mmadi*) of the topology of peace is conserved under all forms of alterations by members as directed by the founder and father of African philosophy, Rev. Fr. Prof. E.M.P. Edeh. The peaceful existence of all members (existing and visitors) of the Pilgrimage Centre for Peace and Reconciliation and the show of charity is well implemented. They all strive for the extension of peace and charity in their homes and extended families. On pilgrimage weeks, for example, thousands of people gather in the Pilgrimage Centre for Peace and Reconciliation topological space seeking solutions to varied problems in order to restore peace in their mind, families, environment, communities, villages, towns, cities and country at large. Sub collections of members of the Pilgrimage Centre for Peace and Reconciliation have been created all over the world extending the ideology of peace and charity as conceived by Edeh and demonstrated in the Pilgrimage Centre for Peace and Reconciliation topological space.

2.3 Convergence in the Pilgrimage Centre for Peace and Reconciliation Topological Space

Generally, convergence in a topological space is easily defined if such a space is metrizeable. In this case, a matrix could be placed on the space. Since the measure of what the Pilgrimage Centre does to millions of people is infinite, the Pilgrimage Centre for Peace and Reconciliation is not metrizeable. As a result, we can only conceive convergence of this space in terms of not metrizeable spaces such as those plausible in Hausdorf topological spaces (Hausdorf, 2002, pp. 91-576). In this light, and like in mathematical topology, there are two types of convergence in the Pilgrimage Centre for Peace and Reconciliation topology: The first typed convergence is disclosed using miracles; mathematically called "duals" or "ideals." Thousands of faithless, solution monster received their miracles as a limit of a filter, through one of the setups of the Pilgrimage Centre.

The second type of convergence is disclosed through testimonies, mathematically referred to as index. Generally, testimonial rites (index) are implemented in the Pilgrimage Centre for Peace and Reconciliation as a start-up point for new intents to be converted. Those who have received solution to their problems explain the steps taken to get their solution and how the Centre helped them to get their solution. Mathematically, if an index of a filter is known, then the convergence of the space is guaranteed.

3. Equivalence between Topology in the Education of Computer Science and Pilgrimage Center for Peace and Reconciliation

Like in mathematics, in the education of computer science, topology refers to the layout of connected devices (shape), i.e. a topology is a network's virtual shape or structure. This shape does not necessarily correspond to the actual physical layout of the devices on the network. For example, the computers on a home local area network may be arranged in a circle in a family room, but it would be highly unlikely to find a ring topology there. Topologies remain an important part of network design theory. You can probably build a home or small business computer network without understanding the difference between a bus design and a star design, but becoming familiar with the standard topologies gives you a better understanding of important networking concepts like hubs, broadcasts, and routes.

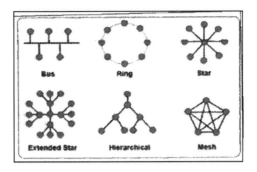

Figure 1: Different topological shapes

A network topology describes the arrangement of systems on a computer network. It defines how the computers, or nodes, within the network are arranged and connected to each other. Computer network topologies (network topologies) are categorized into the following basic types: bus, ring, star, tree, and mesh, while more complex networks can be built as hybrids of two or more of the above basic topologies.

3.1 The Bus Topology and ECP model

Bus networks (not to be confused with the system bus of a computer) use a common backbone to connect all devices. A single cable, the backbone functions as a shared communication medium that devices attach or tap into with an interface connector. A device wanting to communicate with another device on the network sends a broadcast message onto the wire that all other devices see, but only the intended recipient actually accepts and processes the message. Ethernet bus topologies are relatively easy to install and don't require much cabling compared to the alternatives. 10Base-2 (ThinNet) and 10Base-5 (ThickNet) both were popular Ethernet cabling options many years ago for bus topologies. However, bus networks work best with a limited number of devices. If more than a few dozen computers are added to a network bus, performance problems will likely result. In addition, if the backbone cable fails, the entire network effectively becomes unusable. Each node is connected to a central bus that runs along the entire network. All information transmitted across the bus can be received by any system in the network.

As a matter of fact, Edeh and his officiating officers in the Pilgrimage Centre form a Bus through which all communications are sent and received but only the intended structures of the structures receive the specific message.

3.2 The Ring Topology and ECP model

In a ring network, every device has exactly two neighbours for communication purposes. All messages travel through a ring in the same direction (either clockwise or counter clockwise). A failure in any cable or device breaks the loop and can take down the entire network. To implement a ring network, one typically uses FDDI, SONET, or Token Ring technology. Each node is connected to exactly two other nodes, forming a ring. It can be visualized as a circular configuration. It requires at least three nodes. Ring topologies are found in some office buildings or school campuses. The Pilgrimage Centre for Peace and Reconciliation together with all its structures for peace and reconciliation as seen in the charity peace model is a ring topology the removal of anyone of these structures used in establishing peace will certainly lead to remodelling before adjustment. That is, communication will be interrupted before reestablishment, e.g. taking away the university, the Pilgrimage Centre, or the CPM, etc. will certainly have a negative impact on the establishment of peace in the world.

3.3 The Star Topology and ECP model

Many home networks use the star topology. A star network features a central connection point called a hub node that may be a network hub, switch, or router. Devices typically connect to the hub with unshielded twisted pair (UTP) Ethernet. Compared to the bus topology, a star network generally requires more cable, but a failure in any star network cable will only take down one computer's network access and not the entire LAN (If the hub fails, however, the entire network also fails). One central note is connected to each of the other nodes on a network. Similar to a hub connected to the spokes in a wheel. Edeh together with the fathers and sisters of Jesus the Saviour are like a hub in the Pilgrimage Centre. These servants of God together with the institutions of EPTAISM are in a star topology. Communication can only be bridged if the hub is taken out.

3.4 The Tree Topology and ECP model

Tree topologies integrate multiple star topologies together onto a bus. In its simplest form, only hub devices connect directly to the tree bus and each hub functions as the root of a tree of devices. This bus/star hybrid approach supports future expandability of the network much better than a bus (limited in the number of devices due to the broadcast traffic it generates) or a star (limited by the number of hub connection points) alone. In other words, one root node connects to other nodes, which in turn connect to other nodes, forming a tree structure. Information from the root node may have to pass through other nodes to reach the end nodes. The Edeh's charity peace model is conceived from a tree topological perspective. As a tree, Jesus the Saviour is the root from where Edeh stood and implemented all the structures and sub structures of the Pilgrimage Centre for Peace and Reconciliation.

3.5 Mesh Topology and ECP model

Mesh topologies involve the concept of routes. Unlike each of the previous topologies, messages sent on a mesh network can take any of several possible paths from source to destination. (Recall that even in a ring, although two cable paths exist, messages can only travel in one direction.) Some WANs, most notably the Internet, employ mesh routing. A mesh network in which every device connects to every other is called a full mesh. As shown in the illustration below, partial mesh networks also exist in which some devices connect only indirectly to others. As a router, Edeh routs all ideas and benefits that come towards him to the population around using his method of effective charity as described in the ECP model.

3.6 Conclusion of ECP model and Network topologies

The bus, ring, star, tree, and mesh network topologies have been demonstrated in the Pilgrimage Centre for Peace and Reconciliation, which Edeh has used to transform millions of lives. The Pilgrimage Centre for Peace and Reconciliation is not just a topological space in the sense of mathematics but a topological structure for effective communication and restoration of lost hope to individuals and communities. It is therefore a network topology.

4. The Topology of Peace and Education of Computer Science

Before looking at the education of Computer Science in the light of Edeh, we show the following statistics from the World Nation Master 2013.

Table l: Education statistics in Nigeria

Items	Percentage	Position
Adjusted saving: education expenditure > % of GNI	0.85% of GNI	[167th of 168]
Duration of compulsory education	6 years	[149th of 171]
Duration of education > primary level	6	[57th of 181]
Duration of education > secondary level	6	[91st of 181]
Education enrolment by level > Tertiary level	947,538	[26th of 150]
Education, primary completion rate	80	[81st 148]
Female enrolment share > primary level	44.5%	[156th 176]
Female enrolment share> secondary level	45.6%	[129th of 170]
Geographical aptitude results	63.80%	[145th of 191]
Illiteracy rates by sex, aged 15+	31.9%	[35th of 138]
Illiteracy rates by sex, aged 15+ > Women	39%	[37th of 138]
Literacy rates, adult total > % of people ages 15 and above	48.66%	[96th of 121]
Literacy rate, youth female >% of females ages 15 -24	66.47%	[89th of 123]
Literacy rate, youth total >% of females ages 15 -24	73.58%	[86th of 123]
Primary school girls out of school	51%	[22nd of 99]
Public spending on education, total > % of GNP	0.89%	[136th of 136]
Pupil-teacher ratio, primary	37.18	[29th of 159]
Scientific and technical journal articles	384	[53rd of 175]
Tertiary enrollment	4.3%	[116th of 151]
Women to men parity index, as ratio of literacy rates, aged 15-24	0.77	[17th of 138]

(Source: Worldnation Master, 2013)

From the Statistics in education as published in the Worldnation Master in 2013, Table 1 shows that in Nigeria there are 947,538 students in tertiary institutions in Nigeria. Amongst these, over 25,000 are from ECP tertiary institutions accounting for a 0.03%. This is an excellent figure, which could only be compared to some extremely dense states in Nigeria like Lagos.

Out of the over 26,000 graduated students from Madonna University between 2003 and 2013 the institution has transformed some 1600 youths in Computer Science: Computer education has transformed over 90 youths: Computer Science and Information Technology has transformed over 150 youths. Therefore, over 1800 youths have been completely trained in varied computer related disciplines for the information age. Training these individuals, emphasis was on morals, ethics and knowledge. The section on topology of peace in the information age will clearly illustrate this.

5. The Topology of Peace in the Information Age

In this era when the computer has become the centre of every entity, the ideology of Edeh has been highly discussed, is concretely in line with the ethics in the education of computer science. This ethics relates to the ethical values that should guide the computer professionals in their conduct. Ten laws (called Commandments) of Computer Ethics establish guiding principles for all computer users as follows. As specific in Ramon Barquin (1992), every sphere of life is guided by a set of rules of what is right and what is wrong. The difference between the right and the wrong has to be demarcated in any walk of life. With the development of technology and the increase in its use, society had to confront ethical issues relating to the harnessing of technology. The intent behind the creation of these Ten Commandments was to establish a set of standards to instruct people to use computers ethically.

1. Thou shall not use a computer to harm other people.

This commandment makes clear that it is unethical to use a computer to harm another user. It includes harming or corrupting some other user's data or files. The commandment states that it is wrong to steal someone's personal information by means of a computer. It is unethical to manipulate or destroy the files of other people through the use of a computer. It reiterates the fact that writing programs intended to perform ethically wrong actions, is in itself unethical. In the light of Edeh, anybody who contravenes this rule is judged and if found guilty handed to the state for action. No known case to the researcher has been found during this research.

2.   Thou shall not interfere with other people's computer work.

Viruses are small programs built with intent to harm or disrupt the useful computer programs. Some viruses aim at overloading the computer memory by an excessive use of computer resources. These viruses tend to fail a computer in executing the desired tasks. They lead to the dysfunction of a computer. The development or the spread of such malicious software is unethical. This law is observed in Edeh's model with some exception: The department of computer science has developed some viruses in the past for the sake of research since treatment can only come if the source of infection is known.

3.   Thou shall not snoop around in other people's files.

We know that it is wrong to read another person's letters. On similar lines, it is unethical to read another person's email messages. Obtaining another person's private files is as wrong as breaking into someone's room. Snooping around in another person's files or reading someone else's personal messages is the invasion of his/her privacy. In order to protect the information from being attacked, it is ethical to apply encryption schemes to it. This is also a crime in Edeh's charity peace model. In the department of computer science for example, the computer in the laboratories are arranged and setup in a way as to prevent others from moving around others' files. With the conception of designing and implementing a network for the institutions, designers are in the process of taking into consideration these rules. As it is said, "Prevention is better than cure."

4.   Thou shall not use a computer to steal.

The stealing of sensitive information such as the personal information of the employees from an employee database, or breaking into bank accounts for the retrieval of confidential information is nothing less than robbery. An illegal electronic transfer of funds is one type of a fraud. As of now, there exists strict control in place of the methods of payment and withdrawals, and all these can be seen in all the structures of the ECP model. It is known that Edeh does not jump into implementing something because someone uses it but because it will work for him. Structures are in place to control that people do not steal others items (Money or otherwise) or their items stolen. Duping and 419 with the use of the computer does not exist in any of the structures of ECP model.

5. Thou shall not use a computer to bear false witness.

Computers are the easiest sources of spreading information to the masses by means of the Internet. This also means that false news or rumours can spread speedily and easily through the Internet. Being involved in the circulation of incorrect information is unethical. Spreading the wrong information by means of the Internet is like taking an undue advantage of technology. This is controlled in the ECP model. Special content of files to send over the internet are controlled before sending with deactivation of fast data transmission ports (flash port) on public computers in which a centralized server is used to collect mail attachment or downloaded files.

6. Thou shall not use or copy software for which you have not paid.

Like any other artists or literary work, software is also subject to copyrights. Software is the outcome of a programmer's intellect and it is important to respect talent and give due regard to his/her rights. Obtaining illegal copies of copyrighted software is unethical. ECP takes in to consideration this and provides authentic software for all its structures. No computer device is allowed in the Pilgrimage Centre for Peace and Reconciliation without authentic receipts. Some bad elements who wish to breach this role by stealing and throwing over the fence have in the past been caught and resolved accordingly.

7. Thou shall not use other people's computer resources without authorization.

Multi-user systems are supported by user specific ids and passwords. Breaking into some other user's password, thus indulging into his private space on the network is unethical. It is not ethical to hack passwords for gaining an unauthorized access to a password-protected computer system. The ECP model actually and concretely implements this rule on the usage of computer and any other device without authorization. Breaching the security of other people's devices is seen as a crime and settled accordingly. All computer users are advised in ECP model to have strong passwords or other data encryption methods to self-protect their device while security agents have been put in place to guide against defaulters.

8. Thou shall not appropriate other people's intellectual output.

Programs developed by a programmer in an organization are his/her property. Copying them and propagating them in one's own name is unethical. A creative work, a program or a design that a particular employee comes up with, is his/her ownership. It is the output of someone's intellect and efforts. Copying it with selfish intentions is indeed not ethical. The ECP pays for any creative work and doesn't support plagiarism of any kind. Students as well as employees have the opportunity to write or develop software; create hardware and have them keep their authorship.

9. Thou shall think about the social consequences of the program you write.

A computer program goes a long way to reach homes of the masses. In case a person is working for animation films or he/she is designing a video game, it is the programmer's responsibility to pay heed to the effects of his/her creation. In case of software, it is important for the programmer to realize the prospective use of the software. Writing a virus, when one knows that it is going to serve as a malware, is indeed unethical. If a particular content is intended for children or when children are prone to gain access to the content, it is necessary for the creator of such content to be careful about the social consequences it is bound to have. Viewing of adult content is prohibited in the light of ECPM. Members of the Pilgrimage Centre for Peace and Reconciliation are morally driven to keep away from adult contents such as pornographic images and videos.

10. Thou shall use a computer in ways that show consideration and respect.

In the real world, we face situation wherein we need to be courteous to our fellow mates. Many times, we need to cooperate with them and give each of the fellow individuals the consideration due. On similar lines, while interacting through a computer, a person needs to be nice to the ones he/she interacts with. Respect in ECPM is done at all levels. Abusive messages have been traced from their origin on several occasions and settled accordingly.

Therefore, in the information age, where ethics is the key in information transmission, the ECP model has clearly implemented the Ten Commandments of Computer Ethics by putting in place regulations, which are scrupulously followed by its members and subjects. Since the ECP model relies on the set of regulations to guide the individual users (professionals as well) with typically based computer related operations on strong ethical values, it is a model for the information age and should be adopted by the world for effective implementation in this era for a global peace.

11. Hierarchical topology of ECP model

There also exists a hierarchical topology of the concrete realities of Edeh as a structure for connectedness, continuity, boundedness and completeness. The structure shows that Edeh created the Catholic Prayer Ministry, the health establishments and the educational institutions as different branches to establish community peace, sickness peace and illiteracy peace respectively. In the line of setting community peace, Edeh realizes that continuity is required for his agenda to stand the test of time and therefore created the religious men and women of God, which by its own right establishes peace in its own self. He then bounded his teachings by creating the structure of effective peace in which he has a Justice, Reconciliation, Rehabilitation, Charity, Marian devotion, and Museum units that have brought peace to millions of individuals, families, communities, towns, and cities. He connected his community peace structure to health peace structure and illiteracy peace structure for the sake of completeness. Thus, the topology of peace is complete leading to world peace.

12. Discussion and Conclusion

Using structures arranged in all forms of network topologies, Edeh has successfully established peace among millions of individuals and families. The hierarchical topological arrangement of the ECP model shows all the establishments with which this peace has been achieved. As the figure summarizes, he has equally given health to frustrated patients who eventually took the Pilgrimage Centre as their home never to return to their places of birth. He has educated the less privileged, dropouts, quarantines and many others with the numerous lower and higher institutions of learning created. He brought numerous servants of God, for the continuity of the ideologies of peace in a modern world. He confined his subjects within strict borders for eventual maturity before letting them into the society with the training of special security men who adhered strictly to EPTAISM. Unlike other Nigerian men who will not sleep because of terror of armed bandits and house kidnapping in their mind, the Institutions of Edeh offers a fare free society for all, subjects. Being in a non-metrizeable topological space setting, with proven physical convergence properties like miracles and testimonies to millions of lost individuals, the ECP mode should not just be looked upon as a philosophical model with real computational and mathematical properties. Like the statement of Agbo Edmund (2013), in which he said, "Edeh's Model of Peace responds effectively and efficiently to the two dimensions of peace—primordial and secondary—and this response singles it out of other systems or models of peace promoted by other exponents," this model actually captures notions of mathematical topology and computer network topology which may not have been captured by other models of peace. Even though, Ezechi Chukwu (2013) says, "If Edeh has easily solved these millions of cases in his Centre, thereby adding a robust value to human community; it is timely then to integrate this model into the global community in the interest of mankind." This model should be included because it is an innovation in both science and arts. Since the Information Age is universal, and mathematics is the language of science and knows no barrier, this researcher agrees with Oliver Udaya (2013) that, "The model of resolving disputes propounded by Edeh and propagated by his disciples can be effectively applied in any country, creed or context. In other words, it has a universal appeal," and surely and effectively heads to impeccable achievement of World Peace.

CHAPTER TWELVE

EDUCATION AND DEVELOPMENT IN AFRICA: THE ROLE OF FR. EDEH - A LEADING FIGURE IN WORLD PEACE

By Mrs. Kumkum Mathur

Abstract

One cannot hold any reasonable discussion on world peace without bringing Fr. Edeh to the centre of the picture. He very greatly impacts the lives of millions of people, giving them the peace that has eluded them, through his philosophy of thought and action which gave rise to his numerous peace giving establishments.

On 16 May 2013, in Rome, Fr. Edeh was selected as leading figure in the area of World Peace and Global Charity and was given the prestigious award "A Life for Life" in recognition of his activities for the welfare of other lives.

In 2005, Mrs. KumKum Mathur from India stated thus, "By the grace of Almighty God, I came here in Nigeria to join Madonna University as a faculty member in department of Philosophy. During my stay from the year 2005 to 2010, I noticed tremendous development in Madonna University and in the Pilgrimage Center, Elele."

Fr. Edeh has a major role in Education and Development in Africa in diverse ways:

Physically
Socially
Mentally

Spiritually and
Educationally

He is a man, who has through his life and works touched the lives of millions of people and has been described as a "giant of peace for modern world" by the people of Africa.

As a priest, he is gifted with "Effective" Intercession in prayer. No wonder so many people are seen gathering around him and he does for them that which he knows how best to do. That is, giving:

® Peace and consolation to the troubled minds
® Peace to broken homes
® Peace to towns and villages
® Peace to society
® Peace to the Africans
® And indeed peace to the modern world

Establishment of Museum of Charms & Fetish Objects

1. Museum of Charms and Fetish Objects

Charms meant to harm people are so destructive and devastating (like nuclear weapons) while fetish objects are those objects used in the worship of false gods and which are usually planted in people's homes or elsewhere to destroy people. Peace of mankind is usually greatly impaired by the effects of these charms, talismans, and amulets in the destruction of properties and life of mankind in many parts of Asia, and South and Central Africa.

In his method of struggling to create peace for the modern world, Fr. Edeh succeeded in establishing the largest Museum of Charms and Fetish Objects in the world since 1985. Through the retrieval and disempowering of innumerable dangerous charms and fetish objects with which people wreaked havoc in the society, Fr. Edeh has impacted so much to institute peace in the hearts of men because disputes are reconciled by covenants and surrendering of their dangerous charms (voodoos). This then brings unity among the people and enduring peace in the society.

2. Development in Africa by his 'philosophical care', that is, by his work for charity and peace (Edeh's Charity Peace Model) (ECPM) (His work based on philosophy of Igbo-Metaphysics):

By 1984, when Fr. Edeh returned from United States of America to Nigeria after his studies, he was hit by the reality of human life in society where millions of shattered and broken human beings were staggering out of the protracted and devastating Nigerian Civil War (Otherwise known as Biafran War).

In the face of the Civil War, he did not just sit down only to speculate. Rather he went ahead into action, by carrying out his mission of practical and effective charity bringing peace to the world through bringing peace to the individuals, the sick, the suffering, the abjectly poor, and the miserable youths of the society.

For Fr. Edeh, peace is not just the absence of war, rather it is peace that lasts in the presence of factors and forces that eliminate and even prevent conflicts and minimize tensions.

This peace is brought into the society through special and effective charity which provides justice, honesty, education, morality, health, development and respect for the dignity of the human person irrespective of race, color, creed, social status or physical conditions.

Practical and effective charity provides, above all, particular and meticulous care, on one to one basis, of individuals in the category of the sick, the suffering, the handicapped, the lowly, the helpless and the abandoned. Peace is interchangeable with good and love/charity.

Edeh's Charity Peace Model (ECPM) respects and reflects-both the (1) Connatural/primordial and (2) The remedial interpretation of peace.

Edeh's Charity Peace Model is characterized by:

i.   Charity based—Charity rooted in man as "good that is."
ii. It is reconciliatory—an act of bringing together again.
iii. It is mediatory—the mediator is an impartial third party.

iv. It is responsive to both the primordial and secondary dimensions of peace.

v. It is sacramental.

In essence, we say that Edeh's Charity Peace Model is credible and functional, taking into cognizance both the pre and post conflict states of man. Peace is interchangeable with good and love/charity. Peace is attained through love expressed in charity. Charity stands at the center of his thought and action. Peace is the practical expression of charity (love).

Charity/love knows no bounds, the recognition of and respect for human dignity is the simplest way to promote peace.

Edeh's Charity Peace Model re-instates to the human stage the almost, banished presence of God (in human affairs). Human is meaningless without his/her creator. He/she cannot be good if it is not in consonance with good from the supreme 'good that is'.

Fr. Edeh said in his words "my job as a servant leader is to serve the dignity of every human young or old, leader or follower, oppressed or oppressor, local or foreign, black or white, male or female, rich or poor, peaceful or conflicted, educated or illiterate, as possessing the sparks of God".

Edeh's Charity Peace Model has a lot to give to the world. Through his works, Edeh has achieved reconciliation and reconstruction, healing and restoration, repair and resuscitation, dialogue and revival. Interestingly, the end of all these means is nothing other than peace.

Peace to man, peace to the community, as Edeh professes, is all that *mmadi* needs to live the fullness of being as "good that is".

3. Development in Africa by 'Health Care'

For the health care of the abjectly poor and abandoned, Fr. Edeh has worked most assiduously and founded a number of medical institutions to bring health care to the doorsteps of the thousand in the society who cannot help themselves. Some of the Medical Institutions founded are:

i. Our Savior Hospital/Maternity and Rehabilitation Centre, Elele (1986)

ii. Our Savior Motherless Babies' Home, Elele (1992)
iii. Specialist Diagnostic Laboratory, Enugu (2001)
iv. Madonna University Medical Clinic, Okija (2001)
v. Madonna University Teaching Hospital, Elele (2003)

In these medical facilities, the sick, the suffering, the handicapped, etc. are really touched and cared for.

Those who cannot afford any payment are treated and specially cared for free of charge.

4. Development in Africa by 'Educational Care'

Following the devastating Nigeria Civil War- the educational system in the country had almost collapsed giving way to the reign of secret cultism activities, rampant killings and destruction of lives and properties in and around all the tertiary institutions. Students geared by some members of the staff, organize killings of both staff and fellow students. Riots, strikes, and state of chaos and confusion had almost taken over the citadels of learning.

It was in the face of the above circumstances that Fr. Edeh struggled from 1989 till date and established with the government 'approval and certification' of the following tertiary educational institutions:

i. Our Saviour Institute of Science, Agriculture and Technology (OSISATECH Polytechnic) (in 1989).
ii. Our Saviour College of Education (in 1989).

These are the first non-government owned (private) polytechnic and colleges of education in the country.

iii. Madonna University (1999), the first private university in Nigeria and first Catholic university in Nigeria and West Africa.
iv. Caritas University, Enugu (2004)

With the establishment of the above tertiary institutions, the trend of events in the educational sector of the society began to change. Parents can now send their children to any of these institutions and rest assured that they have found institutions where proper education is taken seriously without any problem.

In each of these institutions, Fr. Edeh has extensive scholarship programmes for helpless students who are from very poor parents. Youth who are handicapped, cripples, deaf and dump study on scholarship in these institutions.

5. Development in Africa by 'Religious Care' (Theology) by foundation of religious Men and Women.

In order to perpetuate his practical implementation of African philosophy in real situation, through his mission of practical and effective charity, he like Mother Theresa of India has gone so far as to found some religious men and women, namely:

i.   The Sisters of Jesus the Saviour
ii. The Fathers of Jesus the Saviour
iii. The Male Contemplatives of Jesus the Saviour
iv. The Female Contemplatives of Jesus the Saviour

The members of these religious foundations are trained to implement perpetually his (Fr. Edeh's) mission of practical and effective charity, the realities of African Philosophy.

They are fully engaged in continuing the existence of the Pilgrimage Centre for Peace and Reconciliation, the medical institutions, the educational institutions etc.

Conclusion

As a conclusion of my presentation, I want to say that Fr. Edeh has a great role in the development of Africa and to provide peace to the modern world by

i.   His philosophy of charity and peace.
ii. His health-care providing institutions.
iii. His educational institutions, and
iv. Foundations of religious men and women.

GENERAL CONCLUSION

Among many other factors responsible for lack of peace in the world today, bad leadership, lack of the spirit of charity and improper understanding of the true identity of man stand very prominent.

Funny as it may sound but it still remains a fact that countries do not go to war. The leaders of these countries do. They marshal their reasons, stir up the public, dehumanize the enemy and send out their forces to kill and destroy. It is embarrassing that the number of people actually responsible for the decision to go to wars which have claimed human lives in their millions can comfortably fit inside a single large-sized room.

This is because most of the world leaders, only occasionally represent the interest of the people they govern and majority are not the best of what their society has to offer but got there through abnormalities and so usually exhibit the same failings and weaknesses as seen almost all over the place especially in Africa. They get angry when they should not, let their egos motivate them more than they should, and are entirely too concerned with doing what is popular rather than what is right.

Unfortunately, our world is overtaken by these leaders who see themselves as Lords and consequently ascend to high places from where they lord it over their subjects. This, experiences teach us, has been one of the major factors responsible for wars in our society. Rulers are surrounded by sycophants who tell them what they want to hear and because they are far away from the people, they cannot listen to the genuine voices coming from below.

Consequently, when the people can no longer bear the brunt, they in an attempt to cast off the heavy yoke on their shoulders, resort to violence resulting to most of the rebellions, demonstrations, political unrest, civil war etc that are recorded in the human history.

Edeh in an attempt to arrest this failure in leadership has turned the traditional pyramid of leadership structure upside down, and on the contrary enthrones a leadership structure where the leader places himself at the base considering himself more of a servant than a leader; this gives birth to the Servant Leadership model of Edeh. It is this Servant Leadership structure that Edeh propagates in all his establishments through which he effectively takes proper care of human rights requirements—health care and food for all especially the abjectly poor, handicapped and abandoned, settlement of cases for quarrelling parties, no discrimination for girl child and women in terms of proper moral education and empowerment. This structure of leadership if imbibed by world leaders the history of constant agitation as seen all over the world will be reduced to the barest level leaving our society with the type of peace it deserves.

In addition to the above, the spirit of charity must be imbibed if and only if the world is to experience peace. Today in our world the spirit of brotherhood characterized by charity and support of the vulnerable and the less privileged is gradually making its way to the bottomless abyss. Little wonder, an American psychologist, Thomas Lanten, in his work *Man and Profit Making* puts it that "because man has become intrinsically money conscious and profit oriented, charity has grown cold". Towing the same line but going a little further, one can insist that charity has not only grown cold but it is at the very verge of extinction in our present era. This is because we have lost sight of our moral and philosophical ethos that call for defence of the vulnerable and support of the less privileged. But ironically, this is an era that needs charity more than ever since in our time, war, natural disasters bad governance and other civil disturbances bring about destitution in the human community at an alarming pace. Victims of the aforementioned calamities depend solely on the charity of others to survive; but unfortunately, we now live in a society where before ever people extend a helping hand to others the usual questions are: Who is this person in need of help? Is he/she in any way related to me? What is my own benefit/profit going to be should I carry out this act of charity? If after these questions the answers are not favourable, then such action is not worth going for.

Edeh's charity is therefore aimed at building a world where every human being, no matter his race, religion, societal status, or nationality, can live a full human life, freed from servitude imposed on him or her by other men or by natural forces over which he or she has not sufficient control; a world where human dignity is not an empty idea to the poor. This is a world in which human rights are fully respected, proper health care is available for all, Girl-Child education is taken seriously, there is no discrimination due to gender inequalities, no social instability, a situation where moral education pervades for all in educational institutions. All these are amply brought out in the implementation of Edeh's philosophy based on the understanding of man as *mmadi*. Edeh through implementation of this philosophy using the structure arranged in all network topologies has successfully established peace among millions of individuals and families and will continue to do so in future.

Finally, with Edeh's presentation of man as the good that is as opposed to the ideology of man being a wolf to another, it calls for a change of mentality in our dealings with our fellow human beings who are "goods that are" but not wolves looking for an opportunity to devour each other. With this type of philosophy, the long awaited world peace is certainly being achieved.

BIBLIOGRAPHY

A Jewish conception of Human Dignity. (2006). Philosophy and Its Ethical Implications for Israeli Supreme Court Decisions. *Journal of Religious Ethics 34 (4).*

Agekameh, O. (2001). Guns, Guns Everywhere. *Tell magazine.* August 6.

Alimba, C.N. (2012). Peace, Education, Transformation of Higher Education and Youth Empowerment for Peace in Africa. In A.O. Ayeni, U.G. Emetarom, A.O. Okwori, J.A. Undie and J.E. Okon. *Managing Education for National Transformation* (Ibadan: His Lineage Publishing House NAEAP).

Alimba, C.N. and Awodoyin, O.F. (2008). Disarmament Education Offensive Management of Education for Sustainable Development in Africa. In J.B. Babalola, G.O. Akpa, I. Hausa and A.O. Ayeni (eds) *Managing Education for Sustainable Development in Developing Countries Abuja.* NAEAP/Ibadan: His Lineage Publishing House.

Anumudu, M.U. & Ononuju, N.A. (2011). Gender Inequality: A Cultural Problem in Igbo Land. *Journal of Sociology, Psychology and Anthropology in Practice.* April Vol. 3, No. 1.

Aristotle. (n.d.). Retrieved from www2.cnr.edu/home/bmcmanus/poetics. html

Ayn, R. (1966). The Roots of War. *The Objectivist.* Age Publishing. London.

Bagaric, Mirko and Allan James. (2006). The Vacuous Concept of Dignity. *Journal of Human Rights* 5(2).

Benedict XVI. (July 2006). Homily During the Holy Mass at the Closure of the Valencia World Meeting of Families. Popes' Encyclical.

Booth, P., Tillotson, J. Monoidal closed. (1980). Cartesian closed and convenient categories of topological spaces. Pacific J. Math. 88.

Brown, R. (1973). Sequentially Proper Maps and a Sequential Compactification. *London Math Soc.* (2) 7.

Bull, N.J. (1969). Moral Education. *Routledge and Paul.* London.

Butchman, Frank. (n.d.). Retrieved from www.aabibliography.com/tom_driberg_mystery moral _rearmanent.html

Dahama, O.P., & Bhatnager, O.P. (2005). Education and Communication for Development. 2nd edition. New Delhi.Oxford & IBH Publishing Cp. PW Ltd.

Davis, Julia. (2007). Doing Justice to Dignity in the Criminal Law. *In Perspectives on Human Dignity: A Conversation, edited by J. Malpas and N. Lickiss.* Dordrecht: Springer.

Davis, Marvin. (1976). A Philosophy of Hindu Rank from Rural West Bengal. *Journal of Asian Studies.* 36: pp. 5-24.

Edeh, E. M. P. (1985). Vers Une Metaphysique Igbo. Loyola University Press. United States.

Edeh, E.M.P. (1985). Towards an Igbo Metaphysics. Chicago. Loyola University Press.

Edeh, E.M.P. (2007). Towards an Igbo Metaphysics. Bandury, UK. MinutemanPress.

Edeh, E.M.P. (2006).Peace to the Modern World.Elele, Nigeria.

Edeh, E.M.P. (2007). Peace to the Modern World. Minuteman Press. United Kingdom.

Edeh, E.M.P. (2009). Igbo Metaphysics the First Articulation of African Philosophy of Being. Madonna University Publication.

Edeh, E. M. P. (2011). Philosophy and Social Action in an African Philosophy. Madonna University Press.

Euler, Leonhard. (n.d.). Solutio Problematis ad Geometriam Situs Pertinentis.

Ezeaka, G. (2013).The Nexus of Education and Morality. *Apostles Voice Magazine.*

Ezechi, C. (2013). Actualization of the Millennium Development Goals; Fr. Edeh as a Pacesetter. Madonna University Press, Enugu.

Fafunwa, A.B. (1974). History of Education in Nigeria. London. George Allen.

Fagan, Andrew. (2005). Human Rights. *The Internet Encyclopedia of Philosophy.* ISSN 2161-0002.

Frechet, Maurice. (1906). "Sur quelques points du calcul fonctionnel", *Ph.D. dissertation.*

Frick, E. (2003).Nietzche's Philosophy. London New York.*Continuum.*

Goleman, D. (1995).Emotional Intelligence, U.S.A., Bartam Publishers.

Groff, L. & Smoker, P. (1996). Creating GlobalLocal Cultures of Peace. *Peace and Conflict Studies Journal.* Vol. 3 No. 4 &5

Haralambos, M & Holbron, M. (2008). Sociology. Themes *and Perspectives 7ʰ edition.* London. Herper-Collins Publishers Limited.

Harvis, I. (2004). Peace Education Theory. *Journal of Peace Education.*

Harris, John and John Sulston. (2004). Genetic Equity. *Nature Reviews.* Genetics 5 (10) pp. 796-800.

Hausdorff, Felix. (2002). GrundzOge der Mengenlehre. Leipzig: Veit. In (Hausdorff Werke, II).

John, L. McKenzie. (2002). *Peace* in Dictionary of the Bible. Bangalore. Asian Trading Corporation.

John Paul II. (n.d.). Motherhood, Woman's Gift to Society. Address during the Internal Meeting promoting the well-being of women.

John Paul II. (August 15, 1988). Apostolic Letter, Mulieris Dignitatem. *On the Dignity and Vocation of Women on the Occasion of Marian Year.*

Johnstone, P. T. (1979). On a topological topos. Proc. London Math. Soc. (3) 38, no. 2.

Kant, Immanuel. (1930). Lectures on Ethics. Translated by L. Infield. London. Methuen.

Kant, Immanuel. (1981). Translated by J. Elingeon, Indiana Polis Hakett Publisher.

Kant, Immanuel. (1991). Translated by M. Gregory Cambridge University Press.

Kohlberg, L. (1984).The Psychology of Moral Development. *Essays on Moral Development.* New York: Harper & Row Vol. 2

Kodilnye, G. (2005).Introduction to equity in Nigeria. Ibadan: Spectrum Books Ltd.

Kur, J. T. (2012). The Art of Story-Telling for Child Moral Education in Tinland: Relevance in an Information Age in M. Mboho and H. Batta (eds).*The Companion to Communication and Development Issues.* Uyo: BSM Resources Ltd.

Listing, Johann Benedict. (1848). Vorstudien zur Topologie.*Vandenhoeck und Ruprecht.* Gottingen.

Longman Dictionary of Contemporary English.(1978).

Longman Dictionary of Contemporary English.(2007).

Life and Times of Nelson Mandela. (n.d.). Retrieved from www. nelsonmandela.org.

Macklin, Ruth. (2002). Cloning and Public Policy. *A Companion to Genetics*, edited by J. Burley and J.Harris. Oxford: Blackwell.

Mahatma Gandh. (n.d.). www.biography.com/.../mahatma.gandh

Maralambos, M. with R.M Heald.(1984). Sociology Themes and Perspectives. University Tutorial Press Ltd. Slough SL 1 4JK.

Maria Theresa. (n.d.). Retrieved from www.habsburger.net/en/chapter/ maria.theresa.Great.reformer

King, Martin Luther, Jr. (28 August 1963). I Have a Dream. Retrieved from www.archives.gov/ press/exhibits/dream.speech.pdf

Marrou, H.I. (1966).History of Education in Antiquity. Rome. Stadium.

Mays, E., Analyst.(2011). *Educational Theory of Aristotle.* Available from http: / / www. utm. edu/ research/ iep/ a/ aristotl. Htm.

Mondin, Batista. (1985).Philosophical Anthology. Bangalore. Theological Publication. India.

Narvaez, D. (2006).Integrative ethical Education. Killen. M & Smetana, J.G. (Eds.) *Handbook of Moral Education.* Mahwah, N.J; Erlbaum.

Narayan, D. (2005)."Conceptual Framework and Methodological Challenges", Narayan, D. (ed.) *Measuring Empowerment: Cross Disciplinary Perspectives.* Washington D.C., IBRD/The World Bank.

Nicholas N. C. (Ed). 2012. Edeh's Charity Peace Model. Madonna University Press.

Nickel, James. (2010). Human Rights. *The Stanford Encyclopedia of Philosophy* (Fall 2010 ed.).

Nze C. B. (2011).Aspects of Edeh's Philosophy Vol. 1. Madonna University Press.

Obidi, S. S. (1993). Historical Foundations of education. A. Uba, O. Makinde, D. Adejumo & A. Aladejana (Eds). *Essentials of Educational Foundation and Counselling.* Ile-Ife Department of Educational Foundations. Obafemi Awolowo University.

Odekunle, O. (27 November 2008). Nigeria's Developmental Challenges: Implications for Security. A keynote address to the 9th Annual Colloquium of Ajasin Foundation. Imperial Hall, M.K.O. Abiola Gardens. Ikeja, Nigeria.

Ofer Strichman. (2004).Accelerating Bounded Model Checking of Safety Properties.*Formal Methods in System Design.* 24, pp. 5-24.

Onyewuenyi, Remy N. (2012). The Spatio Socio-Economic Impacts of Emmanuel Edeh's Philosophy of Practical and Effective Charity. *Madonna International Journal* 4 (2).

Onyewuenyi, R. (2010). Very Rev. Fr. Emmanuel M.P. Edeh, C.S.Sp., OFR Man of Peace. His Life and Works. Madonna University Press. Enugu.

Onyewuenyi, R. (2010). Edeh's Philosophy: Philosophy and Society Series, Enugu. Madonna University Press.

Onyewuenyi. R. (Ed).(2011). Edeh's Philosophy: Philosophy and Society Series. Madonna University Press.

Otite, O. (1995).Towards Salvaging a Ravaged Society. Postgraduate interdisciplinary research discourse. University of Ibadan.

Osokoya, I.O. (2012).History and Policy of Nigerian Education in World Perspective. A.O. Ayeni, U.G. Emetarom, A.O. Okori, J.A Undie G.I.E. Okon. Managing Education for National Transformation Ibadan: His Lineage Publishing House: NAEAP Publication.

Plato. (n.d.). Retrieved from www.egs.edu/library/plato/

Poincare, Henri. (1895).Analysis Situs.*Journal de l'Ecole Polytechnique.* Ser 2, 1.

Purissima, E., (2011).Edeh's Philosophy of Being- A Practical and effective Approach. Nze, C.B., (Ed.) *Aspects of Edeh's Philosophy.* Madonna University Press, Enugu.

Purissima, E., December, (2011).A paper presented to the National Council of Women's Societies in Nigeria, Imo State Branch on the occasion of their Annual Women's Leadership Conference.FSP hall, Okigwe Road (Ugwu Orji), Owerri.

Purissima, E. (November 2011). The Philosophical Anthropology of Fr. Edeh: An Essential Pathway to Global Peace. Unpublished Conference paper of International Convention. Elele, Rivers State, Nigeria.

Ramon Barquin. (1992).The Ten Commandments of Computer Ethics. Institute of Ethics in Computer Science. USA.

Sharma, P. (2008). Philosophy of Education. APH Publishing Corporation. New Delhi.

Printed in the United States
By Bookmasters